Graphic Classics:
AMBROSE BIERCE

Graphic Classics® Volume Six

2008

Edited by Tom Pomplun

EUREKA PRODUCTIONS

8778 Oak Grove Road, Mount Horeb, Wisconsin 53572
www.graphicclassics.com

ILLUSTRATION ©2003 STUDIO JAY-BEE

THE OVERLOOKED FACTOR

by Ambrose Bierce / illustrated by Florence Cestac

A man that owned a fine dog, and by a careful selection of its mate had bred a number of animals but a little lower than the angels, fell in love with his washerwoman, married her, and reared a family of dolts.

"Alas!" he exclaimed, contemplating the melancholy result, "had I but chosen a mate for myself with half the care that I did for my dog I should now be a proud and happy father."

"I'm not so sure of that," said the dog, overhearing the lament. "There's a difference, certainly, between your whelps and mine, but I venture to flatter myself that it is not due altogether to the mothers. You and I are not entirely alike ourselves."

CONTENTS

Graphic Classics: AMBROSE BIERCE

ILLUSTRATION ©2008 CARLO VERGARA

Cover illustration by Steven Cerio / Back cover, Page 3 by Carlo Vergara / Page 1 by J.B. Bonivert

Graphic Classics: Ambrose Bierce / ISBN 978-0-9787919-5-7 is published by Eureka Productions. Price US $11.95, CAN $14.50. Available from Eureka Productions, 8778 Oak Grove Road, Mount Horeb, WI 53572. Tom Pomplun, publisher, tom@graphicclassics.com. Eileen Fitzgerald and Lisa Agnew, editorial assistants. Compilation and all original works ©2008 Eureka Productions. Graphic Classics is a registered trademark of Eureka Productions. For ordering information and previews of upcoming volumes visit the Graphic Classics website at http://www.graphicclassics.com. Printed in Canada.

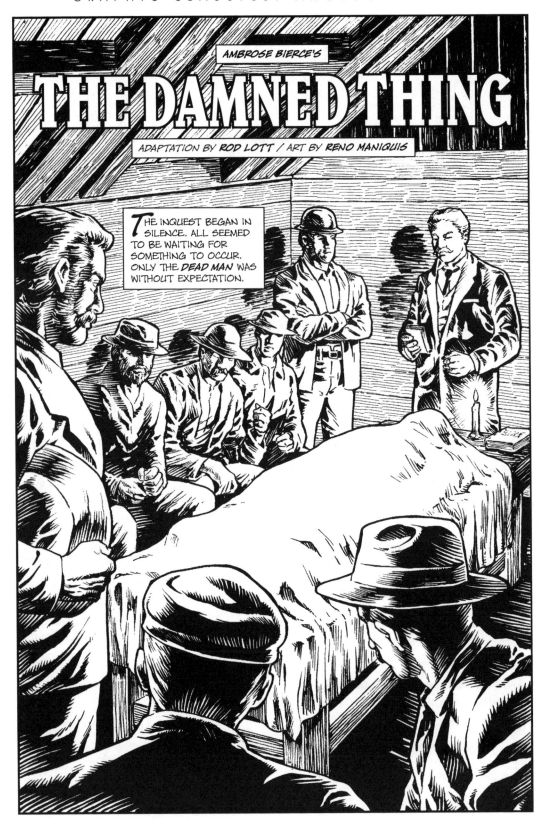

AMBROSE BIERCE'S

THE DAMNED THING

ADAPTATION BY **ROD LOTT** / ART BY **RENO MANIQUIS**

THE INQUEST BEGAN IN SILENCE. ALL SEEMED TO BE WAITING FOR SOMETHING TO OCCUR. ONLY THE *DEAD MAN* WAS WITHOUT EXPECTATION.

THE BOOK HAD BEEN FOUND AMONG THE DEAD MAN'S EFFECTS. BY VIRTUE OF HIS OFFICE, THE CORONER HAD POSSESSION OF IT.

HE CHOSE *NOT* TO SHARE ITS CONTENTS.

THE REPORTER IS HERE.

WE'VE WAITED FOR YOU. IT'S NECESSARY TO HAVE DONE WITH THIS BUSINESS TONIGHT.

SORRY! I WAS POSTING MY ACCOUNT TO MY NEWSPAPER.

THAT ACCOUNT *DIFFERS*, PROBABLY, FROM THAT WHICH YOU WILL GIVE HERE UNDER OATH.

AS YOU PLEASE.

IT WAS NOT WRITTEN AS *NEWS*, BUT AS *FICTION*.

BECAUSE YOU FIND IT *INCREDIBLE?*

NEVERTHELESS, IT IS *TRUE.*

WE WILL RESUME THE INQUEST. NAME AND AGE?

WILLIAM HARKER, 27.

YOU KNEW THE DECEASED, HUGH MORGAN?

YES. I WAS HIS FRIEND.

YOU WERE *WITH* HIM WHEN HE DIED?

NEAR HIM.

RELATE THE CIRCUMSTANCES OF THIS MAN'S DEATH. YOU MAY USE ANY NOTES YOU PLEASE.

"I WAS VISITING HIM AT THIS PLACE TO SHOOT AND FISH. THE SUN HAD HARDLY RISEN WHEN WE LEFT THE HOUSE, LOOKING FOR QUAIL..."

OUR BEST GROUND IS BEYOND THAT RIDGE.

CRRACKKK!!

WE MUST HAVE STARTLED A DEER. I WISH WE'D BROUGHT A RIFLE.

OH, *COME!* YOU'RE NOT GOING TO FILL A DEER WITH *QUAILSHOT*, ARE YOU?

"HE DID NOT REPLY, BUT CATCHING SIGHT OF HIS FACE AS HE TURNED IT SLIGHTLY TOWARD ME, I WAS STRUCK BY THE INTENSITY OF HIS LOOK."

A GRIZZLY?...

"THE SOUNDS HAD CEASED, BUT MORGAN WAS AS ATTENTIVE TO THE PLACE AS BEFORE."

WHAT THE DEVIL IS IT?

THAT DAMNED THING!

"THE WILD OATS IN FRONT OF THE BUSHES STARTED MOVING IN THE MOST INEXPLICABLE WAY, AS IF STIRRED BY A STREAK OF WIND..."

"...WHICH NOT ONLY BENT IT, BUT CRUSHED IT, AND SLOWLY PROLONGED ITSELF TOWARD US."

"I HEARD A LOUD SAVAGE CRY, LIKE THAT OF A WILD ANIMAL."

BLAM!

BLAM!

EEEAACHHH!!

"I WAS THROWN VIOLENTLY TO THE GROUND BY SOMETHING *UNSEEN* IN THE SMOKE."

OOF!

"I HEARD MORGAN CRYING OUT IN MORTAL *AGONY*. MINGLING WITH HIS CRIES WERE HOARSE, SAVAGE SOUNDS. HEAVEN SPARE ME FROM ANOTHER SIGHT LIKE *THAT!*"

NOOOO!!

AAARGGH!!

"HIS RIGHT ARM SEEMED TO LACK THE *HAND*. THE OTHER ARM WAS *INVISIBLE*. IT WAS AS IF HE HAD BEEN PARTLY *BLOTTED OUT!*"

"I SAW AGAIN THE MYSTERIOUS DISTURBANCE OF THE OATS, MOVING AWAY FROM MORGAN TOWARD THE BUSHES."

"WHEN I REACHED HIM, HE WAS *DEAD*."

THE CORONER THEN LIFTED THE SHEET FROM THE DEAD MAN.

BLAUUPPF!

I RECOGNIZE THAT BOOK AS MORGAN'S *DIARY*. I'M SURE IT MUST EXPLAIN —

THE BOOK WILL *NOT* FIGURE IN THIS MATTER, AS ALL THE ENTRIES WERE MADE *BEFORE* THE WRITER'S DEATH.

GENTLEMEN, WE HAVE *NO MORE* EVIDENCE. IF THERE IS NOTHING YOU WISH TO ASK...

ONE QUESTION, MR. CORONER: WHAT *ASYLUM* DID THIS WITNESS *ESCAPE FROM?*

IF YOU PEOPLE ARE DONE *INSULTING* ME, AM I AT LIBERTY TO GO?

YES, PLEASE DO.

THE JURY WILL NOW CONSIDER THEIR VERDICT.

WE, THE JURY, DO FIND THAT THE REMAINS CAME TO THEIR DEATH AT THE HANDS OF A MOUNTAIN LION, BUT SOME OF US THINKS, ALL THE SAME, THEY HAD FITS.

POSTSCRIPT: AN EXPLANATION FROM THE TOMB

IT TOOK SEVERAL MONTHS FOR ME TO GAIN LEGAL POSSESSION OF HUGH MORGAN'S DIARY. I THOUGHT TO MAKE IT PUBLIC, BUT NOW WONDER IF THE CORONER WAS NOT CORRECT IN SUPPRESSING IT.

would run in a circle, ...ut on keeping his head turned away toward the centre, and again he would stand still, barking furiously. At last he ran away into the brush as fast as he could go. I though... ... he had gone mad, b... returning to the house fou... other alteration in his manner than what was obviously due to fear of punishment.

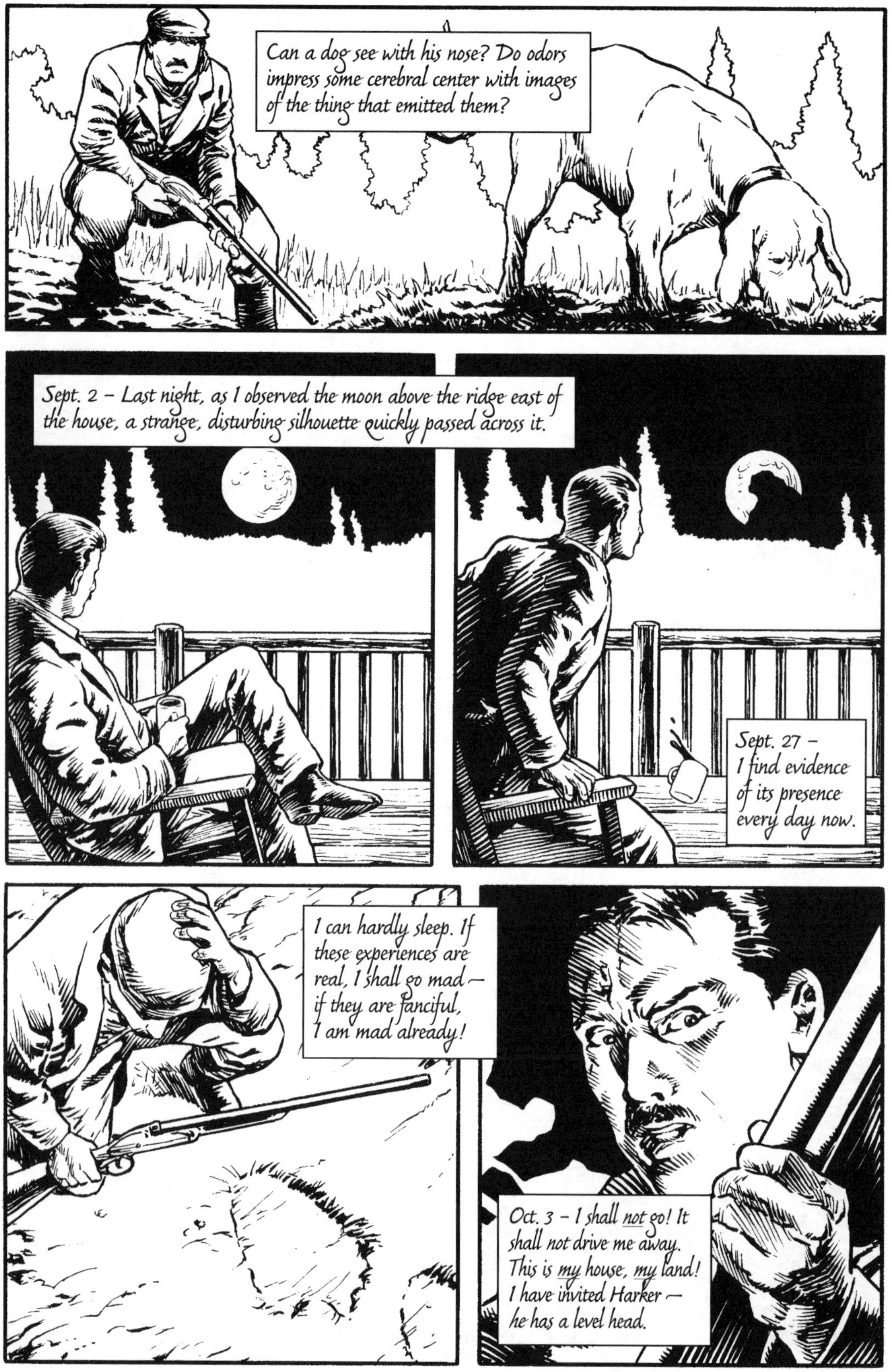
Can a dog see with his nose? Do odors impress some cerebral center with images of the thing that emitted them?
Sept. 2 – Last night, as I observed the moon above the ridge east of the house, a strange, disturbing silhouette quickly passed across it.
Sept. 27 – I find evidence of its presence every day now.
I can hardly sleep. If these experiences are real, I shall go mad – if they are fanciful, I am mad already!
Oct. 3 – I shall not go! It shall not drive me away. This is my house, my land! I have invited Harker – he has a level head.

Oct. 7 – The solution of the mystery came to me last night, as by revelation. How terribly simple!

There are sounds we cannot hear at either end of the scale. I have observed a flock of birds suddenly spring into the air. How? There must have been a signal, unheard by me.

Whales, miles apart, will dive at the same instant. The signal has been sounded, too grave for the ear of the sailor.

As with sounds, so with colors.

I am not mad; at each end of the solar spectrum, there are colors we can't see.

God help me! The Damned Thing is of such a color!

IN OCTOBER 2003 A MARKER WAS DEDICATED AT EASTERN HIGH SCHOOL, MEIGS COUNTY, OHIO.

AMBROSE BIERCE American Writer and Cynic 1842 -???

IT WAS THE FIRST FORMAL RECOGNITION OF AMBROSE BIERCE ANYWHERE.

YOUNGEST OF 10 CHILDREN, AMBROSE GWINETT BIERCE WAS BORN TO MARCUS AND LAURA BIERCE NEAR HORSE CREEK CAVE IN MEIGS COUNTY.

BABE OR BABY, N.- A MISSHAPEN CREATURE OF NO PARTICULAR AGE, SEX OR CONDITION, CHIEFLY REMARKABLE FOR THE VIOLENCE OF THE SYMPATHIES AND ANTIPATHIES IT EXCITES IN OTHERS, ITSELF WITHOUT SENTIMENT OR EMOTION. --AMBROSE BIERCE, THE DEVIL'S DICTIONARY

ONWARD! FORWARD! **CHARGE!**

HEP HEP HEP HEP

HORSE'S ASS

BIERCE WAS A COURAGEOUS SOLDIER DURING THE CIVIL WAR, RISING THROUGH THE RANKS.

FIRST LIEUTENANT BIERCE WAS WOUNDED IN THE HEAD BY A CONFEDERATE SNIPER DURING THE BATTLE OF KENNESAW MOUNTAIN, GEORGIA. THIS NO DOUBT ENCOURAGED HIS SARDONIC WORLD-VIEW.

BIERCE BECAME A NOTED AMERICAN JOURNALIST, FANTASY WRITER, AND CYNIC. HE WAS A FRIEND OF MARK TWAIN AND AN INFLUENCE ON H.L. MENCKEN. HIS SHORT STORY *"AN OCCURRENCE AT OWL CREEK BRIDGE"* IS A CLASSIC OF AMERICAN LETTERS AND *THE DEVIL'S DICTIONARY* STILL PROVIDES QUOTES FOR THE SURLY-MINDED EVERYWHERE.

VALOR, N.- A SOLDIERLY COMPOUND OF VANITY, DUTY AND THE GAMBLER'S HOPE. --AMBROSE BIERCE, THE DEVIL'S DICTIONARY

THE DEVIL'S DICTIONARY

USHER

MOBY

AMBROSE BIERCE

YAK YAK BLAH

BUT THIS ICONOCLAST IS BEST KNOWN FOR...

The DISAPPEARANCE of AMBROSE BIERCE

WRITER: MORT CASTLE
ARTIST: DAN E. BURR
LETTERER: DEBBIE FREIBERG

1913. AMBROSE BIERCE, AGE 71 (PORTRAYED AT THIS AGE BY WOODEN-FACED GREGORY PECK IN THE FILM *OLD GRINGO*). HE HAD MONEY AND LITERARY FAME.

HE ALSO HAD A WIFE WHO DESPISED HIM, AND TWO DEAD SONS -- ONE A SUICIDE, THE OTHER BY ALCOHOL POISONING.

IN A LETTER TO HIS NEPHEW'S WIFE, BIERCE WROTE: "TO BE A GRINGO IN MEXICO - AH, THAT IS EUTHANASIA!"

PANCHO VILLA, BANDIT, DRUNKARD, AND REVOLUTIONARY (PORTRAYED IN 1940 HOLLYWOOD BIO PIC BY WALLACE BEERY)!

BIERCE SAID HE PLANNED TO "HOOK UP WITH PANCHO VILLA" AND SEE "WHAT WAS WHAT."

IT IS THEORIZED THAT "BITTER BIERCE," WHOSE STRONG OPINIONS WERE OFTEN EXPRESSED AS INSULT, ANGERED PANCHO VILLA AND WAS SUMMARILY EUTHANIZED.

I GEEV YOU A DIABLO DICTIONARY, AMIGO!

BLAM
BAM

KILL, V.T. - TO CREATE A VACANCY WITHOUT NOMINATING A SUCCESSOR. - AMBROSE BIERCE, THE DEVIL'S DICTIONARY

BUT THERE ARE OTHER THEORIES. ONE STATES BIERCE NEVER WENT TO MEXICO, BUT ONLY CREATED A RUSE TO COVER HIS SUICIDE AT THE GRAND CANYON.

SHORTLY AFTER HIS "DISAPPEARANCE," BIERCE AND BRITISH ADVENTURER F.A. MITCHELL-HEDGES WERE REPORTEDLY SEEN IN GUATEMALA SEEKING THE ANCIENT MAYAN ARTIFACT CALLED THE *SKULL OF DOOM.*

IT IS THOUGHT THAT BIERCE WENT ON TO BECOME THE "PRISONER-KING" OF A TRIBE OF CENTRAL AMERICAN NATIVES.

KING, N.- A MALE PERSON COMMONLY KNOWN IN AMERICA AS A "CROWNED HEAD," ALTHOUGH HE NEVER WEARS A CROWN AND HAS USUALLY NO HEAD TO SPEAK OF. --AMBROSE BIERCE, THE DEVIL'S DICTIONARY

ANOTHER REPORT HAS BIERCE VOLUNTARILY COMMITTING HIMSELF TO AN INSANE ASYLUM.

MAD, ADJ. ...THIS PRESENT...LEXICOGRAPHER IS NO FIRMER IN THE FAITH OF HIS OWN SANITY THAN IS ANY INMATE OF ANY MADHOUSE IN THE LAND; ...HE MAY REALLY BE BEATING HIS HANDS AGAINST THE WINDOW BARS OF AN ASYLUM AND DECLARING HIMSELF NOAH WEBSTER... -- AMBROSE BIERCE, THE DEVIL'S DICTIONARY

BUT IT WAS THIS MAN, CHARLES HOY FORT, WHO CONCOCTED THE MOST INTRIGUING THEORY TO EXPLAIN BIERCE'S DISAPPEARANCE.

CHARLES FORT IN HIS *BOOK OF THE DAMNED* AND OTHER VOLUMES COLLECTED MORE OR LESS DOCUMENTED EVENTS WHICH SEEMED TO HAVE NO NATURAL EXPLANATIONS, SUCH AS A RAIN OF FROGS.

HIS PIONEERING RESEARCH DIRECTLY INFLUENCED MOST OF THE PSEUDO-DOCUMENTARIES WE SEE ON THE FOX NETWORK TODAY.

LEARNING THAT CANADIAN AMBROSE SMALL HAD MYSTERIOUSLY DISAPPEARED IN 1919, CHARLES FORT IMMEDIATELY UNDERSTOOD THE COMPLEX PLOT.

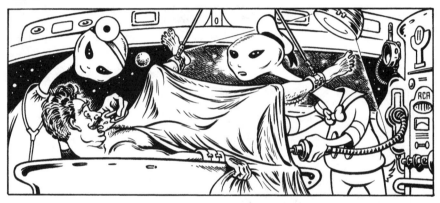

THERE WERE UNEXPLAINED/ OTHERWORLDLY/MARTIANS COLLECTING AMBROSES FOR THEIR (?) OWN ENIGMATIC PURPOSES!

THE ONLY TRUTH OF WHICH WE CAN BE CERTAIN? AMBROSE BIERCE IS DEFINITELY DEAD -- AND SO, DESERVES HIS MARKER IN MEIGS COUNTY, OHIO.

INSCRIPTION, N. - SOMETHING WRITTEN ON ANOTHER THING. INSCRIPTIONS ARE OF MANY KINDS, BUT MOSTLY MEMORIAL... - AMBROSE BIERCE, THE DEVIL'S DICTIONARY.

SO WE WILL LET HIS FRIEND AND DRINKING PARTNER MARK TWAIN OFFER A SUITABLE MEMORIAL FOR AMBROSE BIERCE: PESSIMISM IS ONLY THE NAME THAT MEN OF WEAK NERVE GIVE TO WISDOM.

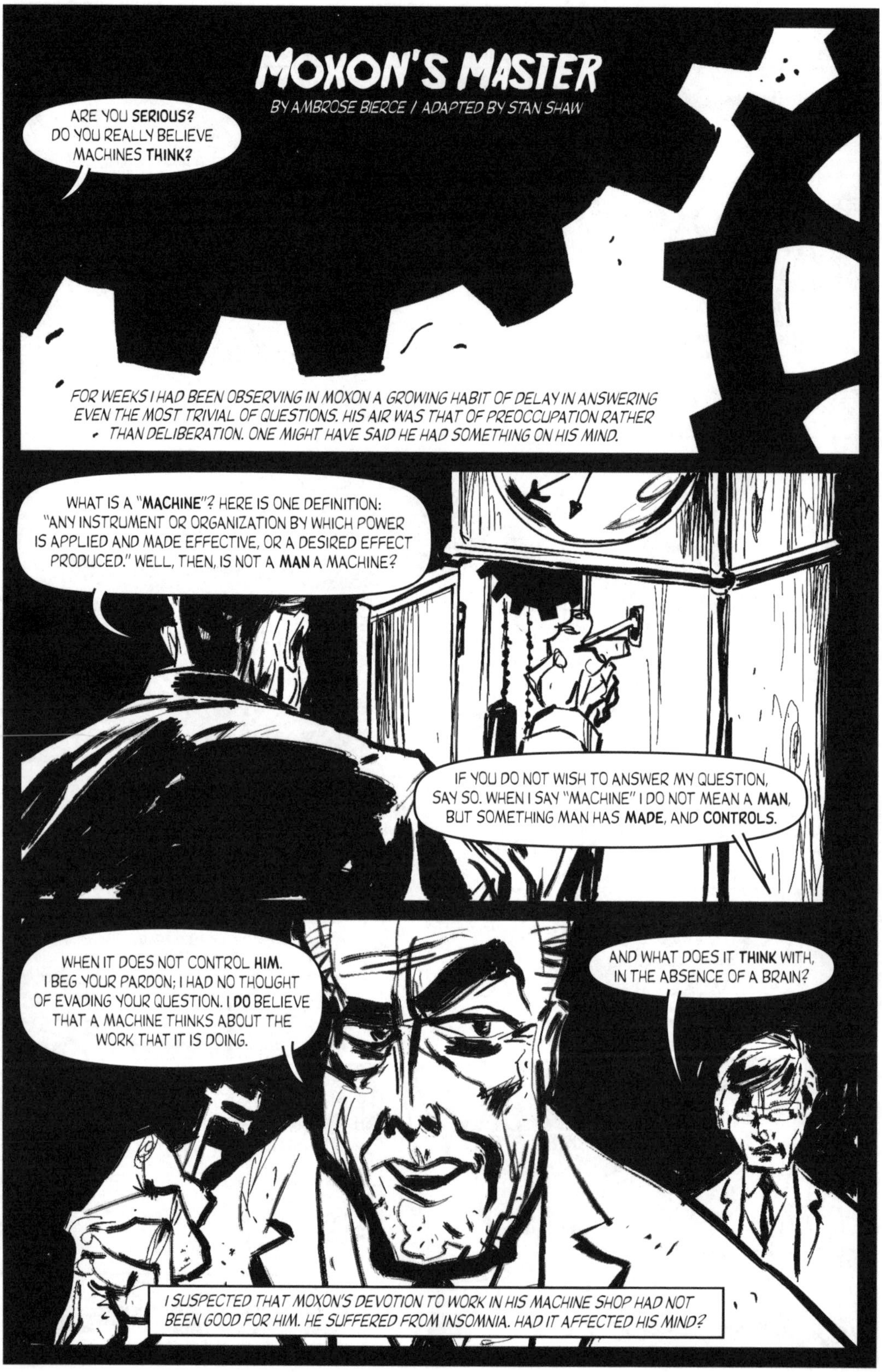
MOXON'S MASTER
BY AMBROSE BIERCE / ADAPTED BY STAN SHAW
ARE YOU SERIOUS? DO YOU REALLY BELIEVE MACHINES THINK?
FOR WEEKS I HAD BEEN OBSERVING IN MOXON A GROWING HABIT OF DELAY IN ANSWERING EVEN THE MOST TRIVIAL OF QUESTIONS. HIS AIR WAS THAT OF PREOCCUPATION RATHER THAN DELIBERATION. ONE MIGHT HAVE SAID HE HAD SOMETHING ON HIS MIND.
WHAT IS A "MACHINE"? HERE IS ONE DEFINITION: "ANY INSTRUMENT OR ORGANIZATION BY WHICH POWER IS APPLIED AND MADE EFFECTIVE, OR A DESIRED EFFECT PRODUCED." WELL, THEN, IS NOT A MAN A MACHINE?
IF YOU DO NOT WISH TO ANSWER MY QUESTION, SAY SO. WHEN I SAY "MACHINE" I DO NOT MEAN A MAN, BUT SOMETHING MAN HAS MADE, AND CONTROLS.
WHEN IT DOES NOT CONTROL HIM. I BEG YOUR PARDON; I HAD NO THOUGHT OF EVADING YOUR QUESTION. I DO BELIEVE THAT A MACHINE THINKS ABOUT THE WORK THAT IT IS DOING.
AND WHAT DOES IT THINK WITH, IN THE ABSENCE OF A BRAIN?
I SUSPECTED THAT MOXON'S DEVOTION TO WORK IN HIS MACHINE SHOP HAD NOT BEEN GOOD FOR HIM. HE SUFFERED FROM INSOMNIA. HAD IT AFFECTED HIS MIND?

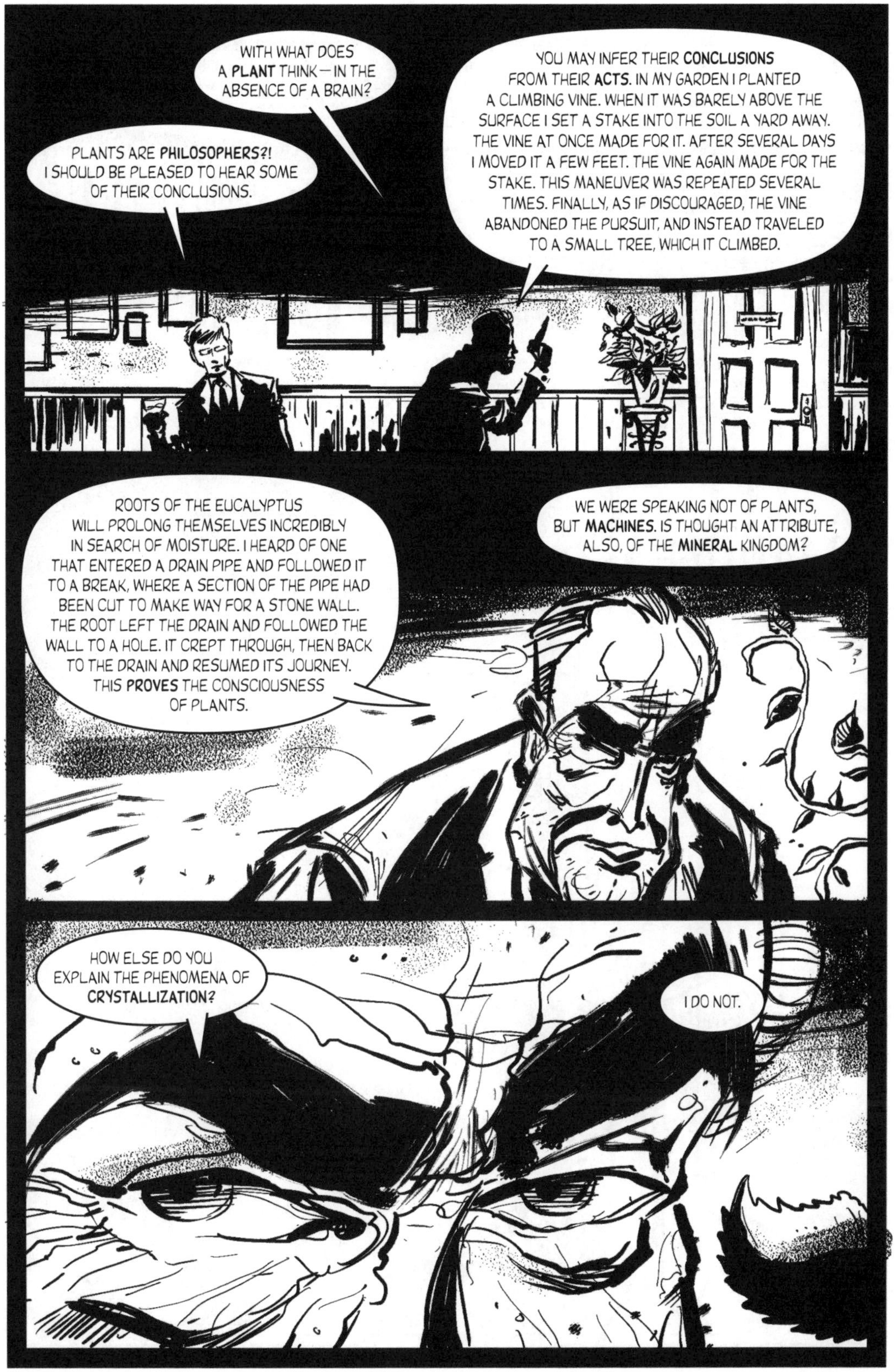
WITH WHAT DOES A PLANT THINK—IN THE ABSENCE OF A BRAIN?
PLANTS ARE PHILOSOPHERS?! I SHOULD BE PLEASED TO HEAR SOME OF THEIR CONCLUSIONS.
YOU MAY INFER THEIR CONCLUSIONS FROM THEIR ACTS. IN MY GARDEN I PLANTED A CLIMBING VINE. WHEN IT WAS BARELY ABOVE THE SURFACE I SET A STAKE INTO THE SOIL A YARD AWAY. THE VINE AT ONCE MADE FOR IT. AFTER SEVERAL DAYS I MOVED IT A FEW FEET. THE VINE AGAIN MADE FOR THE STAKE. THIS MANEUVER WAS REPEATED SEVERAL TIMES. FINALLY, AS IF DISCOURAGED, THE VINE ABANDONED THE PURSUIT, AND INSTEAD TRAVELED TO A SMALL TREE, WHICH IT CLIMBED.
ROOTS OF THE EUCALYPTUS WILL PROLONG THEMSELVES INCREDIBLY IN SEARCH OF MOISTURE. I HEARD OF ONE THAT ENTERED A DRAIN PIPE AND FOLLOWED IT TO A BREAK, WHERE A SECTION OF THE PIPE HAD BEEN CUT TO MAKE WAY FOR A STONE WALL. THE ROOT LEFT THE DRAIN AND FOLLOWED THE WALL TO A HOLE. IT CREPT THROUGH, THEN BACK TO THE DRAIN AND RESUMED ITS JOURNEY. THIS PROVES THE CONSCIOUSNESS OF PLANTS.
WE WERE SPEAKING NOT OF PLANTS, BUT MACHINES. IS THOUGHT AN ATTRIBUTE, ALSO, OF THE MINERAL KINGDOM?
HOW ELSE DO YOU EXPLAIN THE PHENOMENA OF CRYSTALLIZATION?
I DO NOT.

BECAUSE YOU **CANNOT** EXPLAIN WITHOUT AFFIRMING **INTELLIGENT COOPERATION** AMONG THE ELEMENTS OF THE CRYSTALS. WHEN SOLDIERS FORM LINES YOU CALL IT **REASON.** WHEN GEESE FORM THE LETTER 'V' YOU SAY **INSTINCT.** BUT WHEN THE ATOMS OF A MINERAL ARRANGE THEMSELVES INTO SHAPES MATHEMATICALLY PERFECT, OR PARTICLES OF FROZEN MOISTURE FORM SYMMETRICAL AND BEAUTIFUL SNOWFLAKES, YOU HAVE **NOTHING** TO SAY.

AS HE PAUSED, I HEARD IN THE MACHINE SHOP A THUMPING SOUND, AS OF SOMEONE POUNDING UPON A TABLE. MOXON, AGITATED, HURRIED INTO THE ROOM. I THOUGHT IT ODD THAT ANYONE SHOULD BE IN THERE, AS NO ONE BUT MOXON HIMSELF WAS EVER PERMITTED TO ENTER. THERE WERE CONFUSED SOUNDS OF A STRUGGLE, AND THE FLOOR SHOOK. I HEARD HARD BREATHING AND A HOARSELY WHISPERED "DAMN YOU!", THEN SILENCE... PRESENTLY MOXON RETURNED.

MACHINE SHOP

PARDON ME FOR LEAVING SO ABRUPTLY. I HAVE A MACHINE IN THERE THAT LOST ITS TEMPER.

I NOTICED THAT HIS LEFT CHEEK WAS TRAVERSED BY FOUR PARALLEL SCRATCHES, SHOWING BLOOD.

YOU MUST TRIM ITS NAILS.

YOU DO NOT HOLD WITH THOSE WHO THINK THAT ALL MATTER IS SENTIENT — **I DO.** THERE IS NO SUCH THING AS INERT MATTER: IT IS **ALL** ALIVE, AND SUSCEPTIBLE TO THE CONTAGION OF SUPERIOR ORGANISMS, SUCH AS THAT OF MAN WHEN HE IS FASHIONING IT INTO AN INSTRUMENT OF HIS WILL. IT **ABSORBS** SOMETHING OF ITS MAKER'S **INTELLIGENCE** AND **PURPOSE** — MORE IN PROPORTION TO THE COMPLEXITY OF THE MACHINE AND ITS WORK.

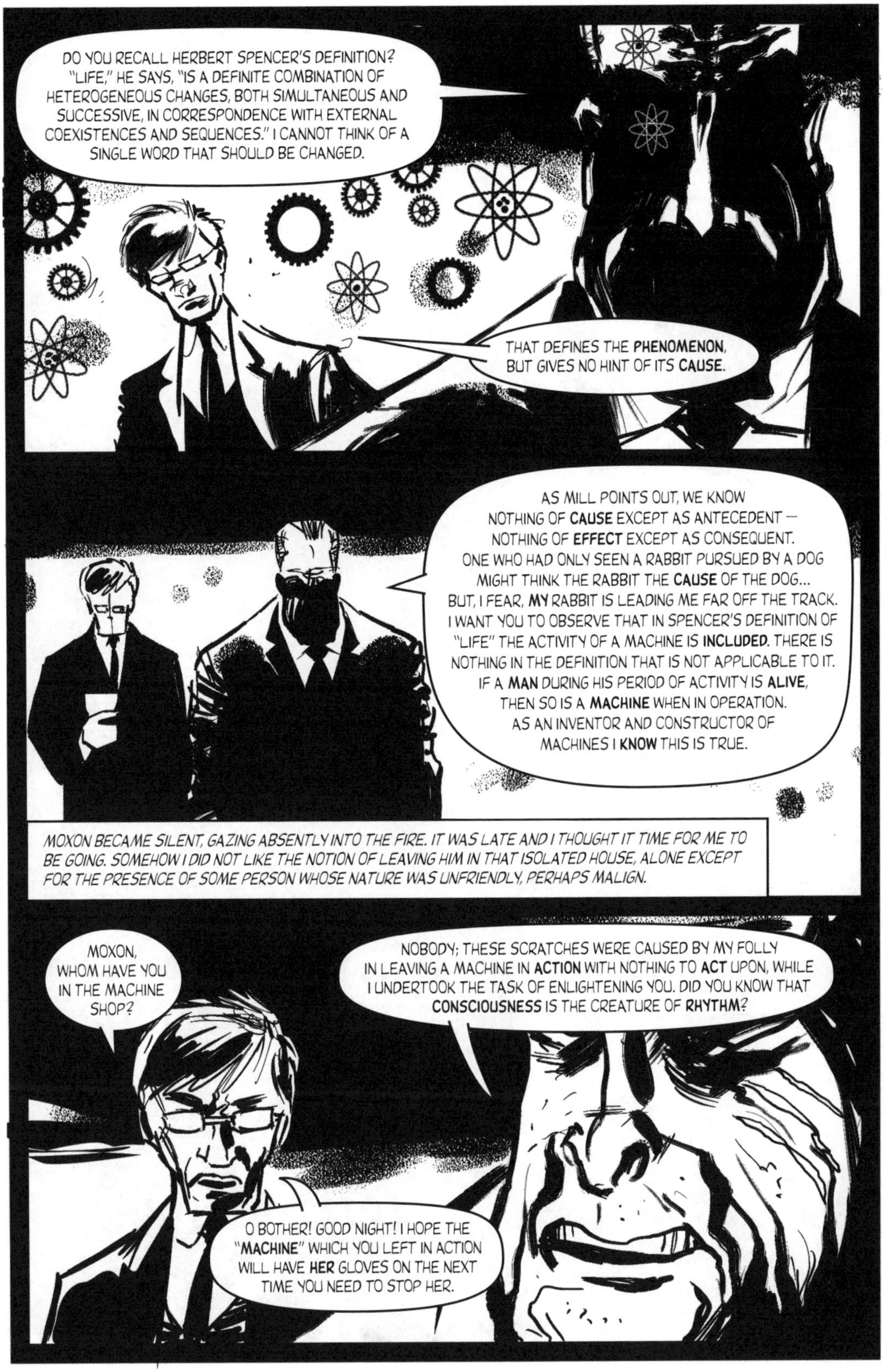
DO YOU RECALL HERBERT SPENCER'S DEFINITION? "LIFE," HE SAYS, "IS A DEFINITE COMBINATION OF HETEROGENEOUS CHANGES, BOTH SIMULTANEOUS AND SUCCESSIVE, IN CORRESPONDENCE WITH EXTERNAL COEXISTENCES AND SEQUENCES." I CANNOT THINK OF A SINGLE WORD THAT SHOULD BE CHANGED.
THAT DEFINES THE **PHENOMENON**, BUT GIVES NO HINT OF ITS **CAUSE**.
AS MILL POINTS OUT, WE KNOW NOTHING OF **CAUSE** EXCEPT AS ANTECEDENT — NOTHING OF **EFFECT** EXCEPT AS CONSEQUENT. ONE WHO HAD ONLY SEEN A RABBIT PURSUED BY A DOG MIGHT THINK THE RABBIT THE **CAUSE** OF THE DOG... BUT, I FEAR, **MY** RABBIT IS LEADING ME FAR OFF THE TRACK. I WANT YOU TO OBSERVE THAT IN SPENCER'S DEFINITION OF "LIFE" THE ACTIVITY OF A MACHINE IS **INCLUDED**. THERE IS NOTHING IN THE DEFINITION THAT IS NOT APPLICABLE TO IT. IF A **MAN** DURING HIS PERIOD OF ACTIVITY IS **ALIVE**, THEN SO IS A **MACHINE** WHEN IN OPERATION. AS AN INVENTOR AND CONSTRUCTOR OF MACHINES I **KNOW** THIS IS TRUE.
MOXON BECAME SILENT, GAZING ABSENTLY INTO THE FIRE. IT WAS LATE AND I THOUGHT IT TIME FOR ME TO BE GOING. SOMEHOW I DID NOT LIKE THE NOTION OF LEAVING HIM IN THAT ISOLATED HOUSE, ALONE EXCEPT FOR THE PRESENCE OF SOME PERSON WHOSE NATURE WAS UNFRIENDLY, PERHAPS MALIGN.
MOXON, WHOM HAVE YOU IN THE MACHINE SHOP?
NOBODY; THESE SCRATCHES WERE CAUSED BY MY FOLLY IN LEAVING A MACHINE IN **ACTION** WITH NOTHING TO **ACT** UPON, WHILE I UNDERTOOK THE TASK OF ENLIGHTENING YOU. DID YOU KNOW THAT **CONSCIOUSNESS** IS THE CREATURE OF **RHYTHM**?
O BOTHER! GOOD NIGHT! I HOPE THE "**MACHINE**" WHICH YOU LEFT IN ACTION WILL HAVE **HER** GLOVES ON THE NEXT TIME YOU NEED TO STOP HER.

WITHOUT WAITING TO OBSERVE THE EFFECT OF MY PARTING SHOT I LEFT THE HOUSE.
I SAW THE GLOW OF THE CITY'S LIGHTS AHEAD IN THE RAIN. BEHIND ME NOTHING WAS VISIBLE BUT THE SINGLE LIGHTED WINDOW OF MOXON'S MACHINE SHOP, AND I KNEW HE HAD RESUMED THE ACTIVITY INTERRUPTED BY HIS DUTY AS MY INSTRUCTOR IN "MECHANICAL CONSCIOUSNESS AND THE FATHERHOOD OF RHYTHM."
AS ODD AS HIS CONVICTIONS SEEMED, I COULD NOT RID MYSELF OF THE FEELING THAT THEY HAD SOME TRAGIC RELATION TO HIS LIFE — PERHAPS TO HIS DESTINY.

I NO LONGER THOUGHT OF HIS VIEWS AS THE VAGARIES OF A DISORDERED MIND. WHATEVER I THOUGHT OF THEM, HIS EXPOSITION WAS LOGICAL. OVER AND OVER, HIS LAST WORDS CAME BACK TO ME, "CONSCIOUSNESS IS THE CREATURE OF RHYTHM." AT EACH RECURRENCE THE STATEMENT BROADENED IN MEANING AND DEEPENED IN SUGGESTION. **HERE** IS SOMETHING UPON WHICH TO FOUND A PHILOSOPHY:
IF CONSCIOUSNESS IS THE PRODUCT OF RHYTHM, **ALL** THINGS ARE CONSCIOUS, FOR ALL HAVE MOTION, AND ALL MOTION IS RHYTHMIC!

I WONDERED IF MOXON UNDERSTOOD THE **SCOPE** OF HIS GENERALIZATION; OR HAD HE ARRIVED AT HIS PHILOSOPHIC FAITH BY THE TORTUOUS ROAD OF OBSERVATION?
HIS EXPOUNDING HAD FAILED TO MAKE ME A CONVERT, BUT NOW A GREAT **LIGHT** SHONE ABOUT ME, AND THERE IN THE STORM AND DARKNESS I EXPERIENCED AN EXCITEMENT OF PHILOSOPHIC THOUGHT! I EXULTED IN A **NEW** KNOWLEDGE, A **NEW** PRIDE OF REASON. MY FEET SEEMED HARDLY TO TOUCH THE EARTH!

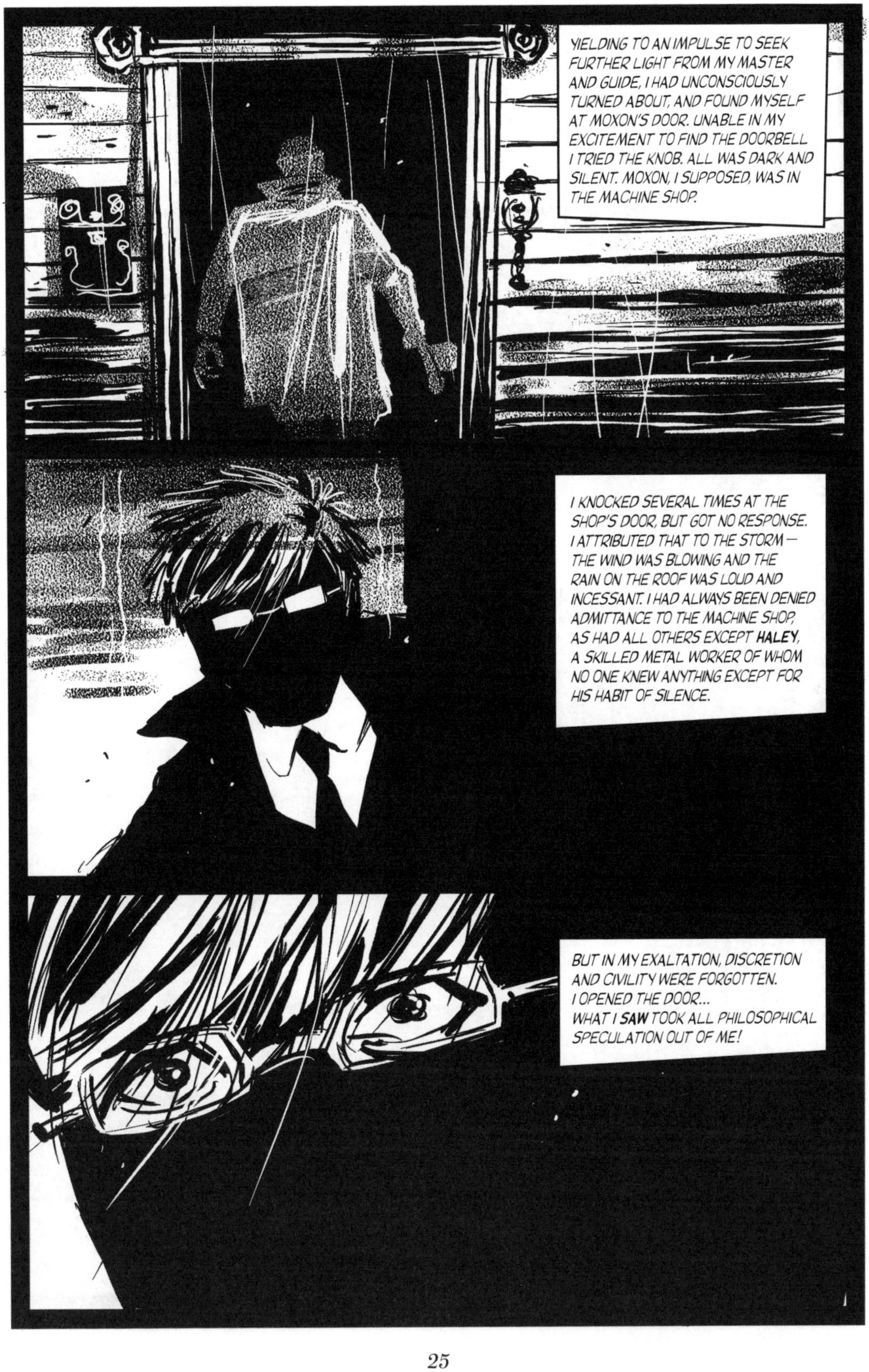
YIELDING TO AN IMPULSE TO SEEK FURTHER LIGHT FROM MY MASTER AND GUIDE, I HAD UNCONSCIOUSLY TURNED ABOUT, AND FOUND MYSELF AT MOXON'S DOOR. UNABLE IN MY EXCITEMENT TO FIND THE DOORBELL I TRIED THE KNOB. ALL WAS DARK AND SILENT. MOXON, I SUPPOSED, WAS IN THE MACHINE SHOP.
I KNOCKED SEVERAL TIMES AT THE SHOP'S DOOR, BUT GOT NO RESPONSE. I ATTRIBUTED THAT TO THE STORM — THE WIND WAS BLOWING AND THE RAIN ON THE ROOF WAS LOUD AND INCESSANT. I HAD ALWAYS BEEN DENIED ADMITTANCE TO THE MACHINE SHOP, AS HAD ALL OTHERS EXCEPT HALEY, A SKILLED METAL WORKER OF WHOM NO ONE KNEW ANYTHING EXCEPT FOR HIS HABIT OF SILENCE.
BUT IN MY EXALTATION, DISCRETION AND CIVILITY WERE FORGOTTEN. I OPENED THE DOOR... WHAT I SAW TOOK ALL PHILOSOPHICAL SPECULATION OUT OF ME!

MOXON SAT AT THE FAR SIDE OF A TABLE. A SINGLE CANDLE WAS ALL THE LIGHT IN THE ROOM. OPPOSITE HIM, HIS BACK TOWARD ME, SAT ANOTHER PERSON. ON THE TABLE WAS A CHESS BOARD. MOXON APPEARED TO BE INTENSELY INTERESTED, NOT SO MUCH IN THE **GAME**, AS IN HIS **ANTAGONIST**. HE WAS SO FIXED ON HIS OPPONENT THAT, THOUGH I WAS DIRECTLY IN HIS LINE OF VISION, I WAS ALTOGETHER UNOBSERVED.

OF HIS ANTAGONIST I HAD ONLY A BACK VIEW. I SHOULD **NOT** HAVE CARED TO SEE HIS **FACE**. HE WAS NOT MORE THAN FIVE FEET TALL, WITH PROPORTIONS SUGGESTING A GORILLA; TREMENDOUSLY WIDE SHOULDERS, THICK, SHORT NECK AND BROAD, SQUAT HEAD, WITH A TANGLED GROWTH OF BLACK HAIR TOPPED WITH A FEZ. A TUNIC BELTED TIGHTLY AT THE WAIST REACHED THE BOX UPON WHICH HE SAT. HIS LEGS AND FEET WERE HIDDEN. HIS LEFT ARM RESTED IN HIS LAP. HE MOVED HIS PIECES WITH HIS RIGHT HAND, WHICH SEEMED DISPROPORTIONATELY LONG.

I STOOD BY THE DOORWAY IN SHADOW, TRANSFIXED BY A FEELING THAT I WAS IN THE PRESENCE OF IMMINENT TRAGEDY.

THE PLAY WAS RAPID. MOXON HARDLY GLANCED AT THE BOARD. HE SEEMED TO MOVE THE PIECE MOST CONVENIENT TO HIS HAND, HIS MOTIONS QUICK, NERVOUS AND LACKING IN PRECISION. THE RESPONSE OF HIS ANTAGONIST, WAS EQUALLY PROMPT IN INCEPTION, BUT MADE WITH A SLOW, MECHANICAL AND SOMEWHAT THEATRICAL MOVEMENT OF THE ARM. THERE SEEMED SOMETHING **UNEARTHLY** ABOUT IT ALL.

A FEW TIMES AFTER MOVING A PIECE THE STRANGER INCLINED HIS HEAD, AND EACH TIME I OBSERVED THAT MOXON SHIFTED HIS KING. THE THOUGHT CAME TO ME THAT THE MAN WAS DUMB — AND THEN THAT **HE WAS A MACHINE!** — **AN AUTOMATON CHESS-PLAYER!** MOXON HAD ONCE SPOKEN ABOUT SUCH A MECHANISM, THOUGH I DID NOT KNOW THAT IT HAD ACTUALLY BEEN CONSTRUCTED. WAS ALL HIS TALK ABOUT THE CONSCIOUSNESS AND INTELLIGENCE OF MACHINES BUT A PRELUDE TO THE EXHIBITION OF THIS DEVICE?

A FINE END TO ALL MY INTELLECTUAL TRANSPORTS AND EXCITEMENT OF PHILOSOPHIC THOUGHT! I WAS ABOUT TO RETIRE IN DISGUST WHEN THE THING'S GREAT SHOULDERS SHRUGGED, AS IF IRRITATED. THE MOVEMENT WAS SO NATURAL, AND SO ENTIRELY HUMAN, THAT IT STARTLED ME. THEN IT STRUCK THE TABLE WITH ITS CLENCHED HAND, A GESTURE THAT APPEARED TO STARTLE MOXON EVEN MORE THAN ME.

THE PLAY RESUMED UNTIL MOXON MOVED ONE OF HIS PIECES AND EXCLAIMED *"CHECK-MATE!"* HE ROSE QUICKLY TO HIS FEET AND STEPPED BEHIND HIS CHAIR.

THE AUTOMATON SAT MOTIONLESS.

THE STORM OUTSIDE CONTINUED, AND IN THE PAUSES BETWEEN THUNDER I BECAME CONSCIOUS OF A LOW BUZZING WHICH GREW CONTINUALLY LOUDER. IT CAME FROM THE **AUTOMATON** — AN UNMISTAKABLE WHIRRING OF WHEELS, LIKE THOSE OF A DISORDERED MECHANISM. A CONVULSION THEN TOOK POSSESSION OF THE MACHINE, AND IT SHOOK LIKE A MAN WITH PALSY. THE ENTIRE FIGURE WAS IN VIOLENT AGITATION.

SUDDENLY IT SPRANG TO ITS FEET AND SHOT FORWARD WITH BOTH ARMS THRUST FORTH. MOXON THREW HIMSELF BACKWARD, BUT HE WAS TOO LATE! I SAW THE THING'S **HAND** CLOSE ON HIS **THROAT!** THE TABLE WAS OVERTURNED, THE CANDLE EXTINGUISHED, AND ALL WAS PITCH BLACK. I RUSHED TO MY FRIEND'S RESCUE, GUIDED BY THE NOISE OF THE STRUGGLE AND MOXON'S FAILING EFFORT TO BREATHE!

HARDLY HAD I TAKEN A STRIDE WHEN THERE CAME A FLASH, AND THE ROOM BLAZED WITH A BLINDING LIGHT THAT BURNED INTO MY BRAIN A VIVID PICTURE OF THE COMBATANTS. I *STILL* SEE MOXON, HIS THROAT IN THE CLUTCH OF THOSE IRON HANDS... HIS HEAD FORCED BACK, EYES PROTRUDING, AND MOUTH WIDE OPEN!

...AND, IN HORRIBLE CONTRAST, UPON THE PAINTED FACE OF HIS ASSASSIN AN EXPRESSION OF TRANQUIL THOUGHT, AS IN THE SOLUTION OF A CHESS PROBLEM!

THEN ALL WAS BLACKNESS AND SILENCE.

THREE DAYS LATER I AWOKE IN A HOSPITAL. AS THE MEMORY OF THAT NIGHT SLOWLY RETURNED, I RECOGNIZED AS MY VISITOR MOXON'S CONFIDENTIAL WORKMAN, HALEY.

TELL ME WHAT HAPPENED.

YOU WERE CARRIED, UNCONSCIOUS, FROM A BURNING HOUSE — MOXON'S. THE ORIGIN OF THE FIRE IS A BIT MYSTERIOUS. MY OWN NOTION IS THAT THE HOUSE WAS STRUCK BY **LIGHTNING**.

AND MOXON?

BURIED YESTERDAY — WHAT WAS **LEFT** OF HIM.

WHO RESCUED ME?

IF THAT INTERESTS YOU, I DID.

THANK YOU, MR. HALEY. DID YOU RESCUE, ALSO, THAT CHARMING PRODUCT OF YOUR SKILL, THE AUTOMATON CHESS-PLAYER THAT **MURDERED** ITS INVENTOR?

THE MAN WAS SILENT A LONG TIME, LOOKING AWAY FROM ME. PRESENTLY HE TURNED AND GRAVELY SPOKE...

DO YOU **KNOW** THAT?

I **DO**, I SAW IT DONE.

THAT WAS MANY YEARS AGO. IF ASKED TODAY I SHOULD ANSWER LESS CONFIDENTLY.

THE STRANGER

a story by **Ambrose Bierce** illustrated by **Mark A. Nelson**

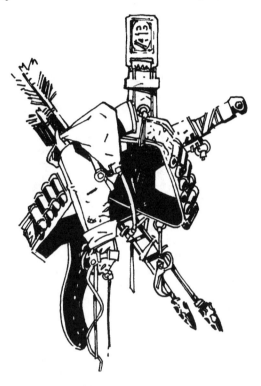

A man stepped out of the darkness into the little illuminated circle about our failing campfire and said gravely...

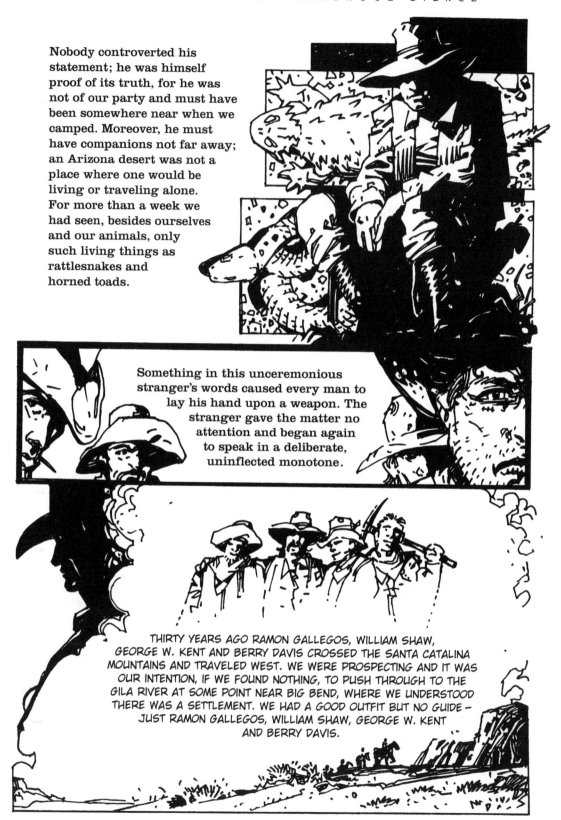

Nobody controverted his statement; he was himself proof of its truth, for he was not of our party and must have been somewhere near when we camped. Moreover, he must have companions not far away; an Arizona desert was not a place where one would be living or traveling alone. For more than a week we had seen, besides ourselves and our animals, only such living things as rattlesnakes and horned toads.

Something in this unceremonious stranger's words caused every man to lay his hand upon a weapon. The stranger gave the matter no attention and began again to speak in a deliberate, uninflected monotone.

THIRTY YEARS AGO RAMON GALLEGOS, WILLIAM SHAW, GEORGE W. KENT AND BERRY DAVIS CROSSED THE SANTA CATALINA MOUNTAINS AND TRAVELED WEST. WE WERE PROSPECTING AND IT WAS OUR INTENTION, IF WE FOUND NOTHING, TO PUSH THROUGH TO THE GILA RIVER AT SOME POINT NEAR BIG BEND, WHERE WE UNDERSTOOD THERE WAS A SETTLEMENT. WE HAD A GOOD OUTFIT BUT NO GUIDE — JUST RAMON GALLEGOS, WILLIAM SHAW, GEORGE W. KENT AND BERRY DAVIS.

The man repeated the names slowly and distinctly, as if to fix them in the memories of his audience. We knew that the solitary life of many a plainsman had a tendency to develop eccentricities not always distinguishable from mental aberration.

A man is like a tree: in a forest of his fellows he will grow as straight as his nature permits; alone, he yields to the stresses and tortions that environ him.

Having undertaken to tell this story, I wish that I could describe the man's appearance. Strangely, I find myself unable to do so with any degree of confidence, for afterward no two of us agreed as to what he wore and how he looked; and when I try to set down my own impressions they elude me.

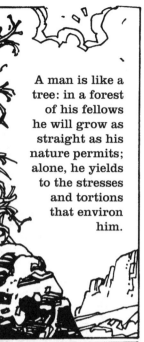

THIS COUNTRY WAS NOT THEN WHAT IT IS NOW. THERE WAS LITTLE GAME HERE AND THE WATER HOLES WERE INFREQUENT. WITHIN A WEEK THE PURPOSE OF THE EXPEDITION HAD ALTERED FROM DISCOVERY OF WEALTH TO PRESERVATION OF LIFE. WE HAD GONE TOO FAR TO GO BACK, SO WE PUSHED ON, RIDING BY NIGHT TO AVOID INDIANS AND THE INTOLERABLE HEAT, AND CONCEALING OURSELVES BY DAY AS BEST WE COULD.

SOMETIMES, HAVING EXHAUSTED OUR SUPPLIES, WE WERE DAYS WITHOUT FOOD OR DRINK; THEN A WATER HOLE OR A SHALLOW POOL SO RESTORED OUR STRENGTH AND SANITY THAT WE WERE ABLE TO SHOOT A BEAR, AN ANTELOPE, A COYOTE, OR A COUGAR – ALL WERE FOOD.

ONE MORNING AS WE SKIRTED A MOUNTAIN RANGE, SEEKING A PRACTICABLE PASS, WE WERE ATTACKED BY A BAND OF APACHES WHO HAD FOLLOWED OUR TRAIL. KNOWING THAT THEY OUTNUMBERED US TEN TO ONE, THEY DASHED UPON US AT A GALLOP, FIRING AND YELLING. FIGHTING WAS OUT OF THE QUESTION. WE URGED OUR FEEBLE ANIMALS UP THE GULCH AS FAR AS THERE WAS FOOTING, THEN THREW OURSELVES OUT OF OUR SADDLES, ABANDONING OUR ENTIRE OUTFIT TO THE ENEMY. BUT WE RETAINED OUR RIFLES, EVERY MAN – RAMON GALLEGOS, WILLIAM SHAW, GEORGE W. KENT AND BERRY DAVIS.

SAME OLD CROWD.

A gesture of disapproval from our leader silenced the humorist and the stranger proceeded with his tale.

TWENTY YARDS UP THE SLOPE, BEYOND THE EDGE OF THE BRUSH, WERE VERTICAL CLIFFS, IN WHICH, DIRECTLY IN FRONT OF US, WAS A NARROW OPENING. INTO THAT WE RAN, FINDING OURSELVES IN A LARGE CAVERN.

HERE FOR A TIME WE WERE SAFE: A SINGLE MAN WITH A RIFLE COULD DEFEND THE ENTRANCE AGAINST ALL THE APACHES IN THE LAND. BUT AGAINST HUNGER AND THIRST WE HAD NO DEFENSE.

BY DAY AND BY NIGHT THE INDIANS WATCHED WITH READY RIFLES. NOT A MAN OF US WOULD LIVE TO STEP INTO THE OPEN. FOR THREE DAYS WE HELD OUT. THEN, IN THE MORNING OF THE FOURTH DAY, RAMON GALLEGOS SPOKE.

"PARDON, SENORES, IF I SHOCK YOU, BUT FOR ME THE TIME IS COME TO BEAT THE GAME OF THE APACHE."

HE KNELT UPON THE FLOOR OF THE CAVE AND PRESSED HIS PISTOL AGAINST HIS TEMPLE.
"MADRE DE DIOS," HE SAID, "COMES NOW THE SOUL OF RAMON GALLEGOS."

"HE WAS A BRAVE MAN," I SAID. "HE KNEW WHEN TO DIE, AND HOW. IT IS FOOLISH TO GO MAD FROM THIRST, OR BE SKINNED ALIVE. LET US JOIN RAMON GALLEGOS."
"THAT IS RIGHT," SAID WILLIAM SHAW.
"THAT IS RIGHT," SAID GEORGE W. KENT.
"IT SHALL BE SO," I SAID.

"WILLIAM SHAW AND GEORGE W. KENT, DRAW AND KNEEL."

"ALMIGHTY GOD, FORGIVE US OUR SINS," SAID WILLIAM SHAW.

"RECEIVE OUR SOULS," SAID GEORGE W. KENT.

"AMEN." SAID I.

I LAID THEM BESIDE RAMON GALLEGOS AND COVERED THEIR FACES.

There was a quick commotion on the opposite side of the campfire...

AND *YOU*! YOU DARED TO *ESCAPE*? *YOU DARE TO BE ALIVE*? I'LL SEND YOU TO JOIN THEM IF I HANG FOR IT!

HOLD IT IN, SAM YOUNTSEY!

CAPTAIN, THERE IS SOMETHING *WRONG* HERE. THIS FELLOW IS EITHER A LUNATIC OR MERELY A LIAR. IF THIS MAN WAS OF THAT PARTY IT HAD *FIVE MEMBERS*.

YES, THERE IS SOMETHING – UNUSUAL. YEARS AGO FOUR BODIES, SCALPED AND MUTILATED, WERE FOUND ABOUT THE MOUTH OF THAT CAVE. THEY ARE BURIED THERE; I HAVE SEEN THE GRAVES.

The stranger rose, standing tall in the light of the expiring fire.

THERE WERE FOUR. RAMON GALLEGOS, WILLIAM SHAW, GEORGE W. KENT AND BERRY DAVIS.

He walked into the darkness and we saw him no more.

At that moment the man who had been on guard strode in.

WHO THE DEVIL DO YOU TAKE THEM TO BE?

RAMON GALLEGOS, WILLIAM SHAW AND GEORGE W. KENT.

CAPTAIN! FOR THE LAST HALF-HOUR THREE MEN HAVE BEEN STANDING OUT ON THE MESA!

BUT HOW ABOUT BERRY DAVIS? I OUGHT TO HAVE SHOT HIM!

QUITE NEEDLESS; YOU COULDN'T HAVE MADE HIM ANY DEADER.

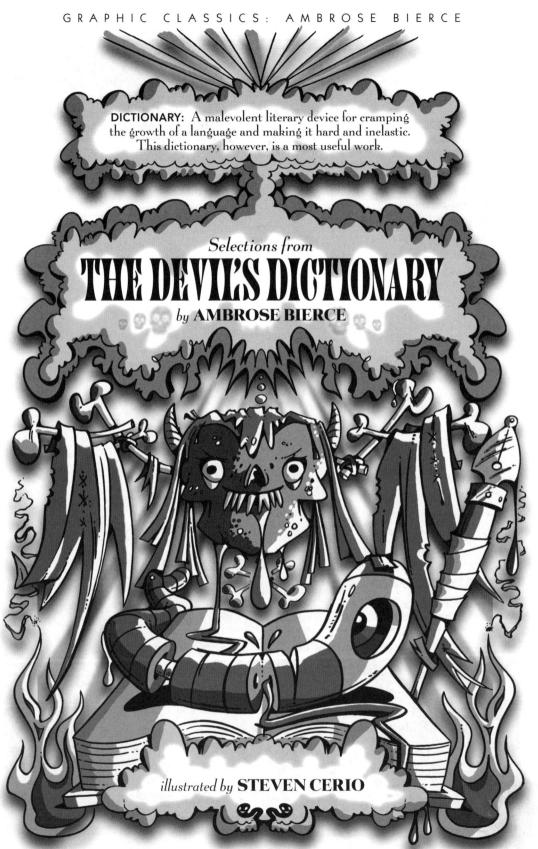

DICTIONARY: A malevolent literary device for cramping the growth of a language and making it hard and inelastic. This dictionary, however, is a most useful work.

Selections from

THE DEVIL'S DICTIONARY

by **AMBROSE BIERCE**

illustrated by **STEVEN CERIO**

ABSURDITY: A statement or belief manifestly inconsistent with one's own opinion.

ACQUAINTANCE: A person whom we know well enough to borrow from, but not well enough to lend to.

ADMIRATION: Our polite recognition of another's resemblance to ourselves.

ADORE: To venerate expectantly.

ALLIANCE: In international politics, the union of two thieves who have their hands so deeply inserted in each other's pockets that they cannot separately plunder a third.

AMBITION: An overmastering desire to be vilified by enemies while living and made ridiculous by friends when dead.

AMNESTY: The state's magnanimity to those offenders whom it would be too expensive to punish.

APOLOGIZE: To lay the foundation for a future offense.

ARCHITECT: One who drafts a plan of your house, and plans a draft of your money.

BACK: That part of your friend which it is your privilege to contemplate in your adversity.

BAROMETER: An ingenious instrument which indicates what kind of weather we are having.

BATTLE: A method of untying with the teeth a political knot that would not yield to the tongue.

BEGGAR: One who has relied on the assistance of his friends.

BELLADONNA: In Italian a beautiful lady; in English a deadly poison. A striking example of the essential identity of the two tongues.

BIGAMY: A mistake in taste for which the wisdom of the future will adjudge a punishment called trigamy.

BIGOT: One who is obstinately and zealously attached to an opinion that you do not entertain.

BIRTH: The first and direst of all disasters.

BLANK-VERSE: Unrhymed iambic pentameters — the most difficult kind of English verse to write acceptably; a kind, therefore, much affected by those who cannot acceptably write any kind.

BODY-SNATCHER: One who supplies the young physicians with that with which the old physicians have supplied the undertaker.

BORE: A person who talks when you wish him to listen.

BOUNDARY: An imaginary line between two nations, separating the imaginary rights of one from the imaginary rights of the other.

BRIDE: A woman with a fine prospect of happiness behind her.

CABBAGE: A familiar garden vegetable about as large and wise as a man's head.

CEMETERY: An isolated suburban spot where mourners match lies, poets write at a target and stone-cutters spell for a wager.

CENTAUR: One of a race of persons who lived before the division of labor had been carried to such a pitch of differentiation.

CHILDHOOD: The period of human life intermediate between the idiocy of infancy and the folly of youth — two removes from the sin of manhood and three from the remorse of age.

CHRISTIAN: One who believes that the New Testament is a divinely inspired book admirably suited to the spiritual needs of his neighbor.

CLERGYMAN: A man who undertakes the management of our spiritual affairs as a method of bettering his temporal ones.

COMMERCE: A kind of transaction in which A plunders from B the goods of C, and for compensation B picks the pocket of D of money belonging to E.

CONSERVATIVE: A statesman who is enamored of existing evils, as distinguished from the Liberal, who wishes to replace them with others.

CONSULT: To seek another's approval of a course already decided on.

CONVERSATION: A fair to the display of the minor mental commodities, each exhibitor being too intent upon the arrangement of his own wares to observe those of his neighbor.

CORPORATION: An ingenious device for obtaining individual profit without individual responsibility.

BAIT: A preparation that renders the hook more palatable. The best kind is beauty.

DANCE: To leap about to the sound of tittering music, preferably with arms about your neighbor's wife or daughter.

DENTIST: A prestidigitator who, putting metal into your mouth, pulls coins out of your pocket.

DESTINY: A tyrant's authority for crime and fool's excuse for failure.

DIAPHRAGM: A muscular partition separating disorders of the chest from disorders of the bowels.

DIPLOMACY: The patriotic art of lying for one's country.

DISTANCE: The only thing that the rich are willing for the poor to call theirs, and keep.

DUTY: That which sternly impels us in the direction of profit, along the line of desire.

EDIBLE: Good to eat, and wholesome to digest, as a worm to a toad, a toad to a snake, a snake to a pig, a pig to a man, and a man to a worm.

EGOTIST: A person of low taste, more interested in himself than in me.

EXPERIENCE: The wisdom that enables us to recognize as an undesirable old acquaintance the folly that we have already embraced.

FAITH: Belief without evidence in what is told by one who speaks without knowledge, of things without parallel.

FASHION: A despot whom the wise ridicule and obey.

FLY-SPECK: The prototype of punctuation. Fully to understand the important services that flies perform to literature it is only necessary to lay a page of some popular novelist alongside a saucer of cream-and-molasses in a sunny room and observe "how the wit brightens and the style refines" in accurate proportion to the duration of exposure.

FREEDOM: A political condition that every nation supposes itself to enjoy in virtual monopoly. The distinction between freedom and liberty is not accurately known; naturalists have never been able to find a living specimen of either.

FRIENDSHIP: A ship big enough to carry two in fair weather, but only one in foul.

FUNERAL: A pageant whereby we attest our respect for the dead by enriching the undertaker.

GHOST: The outward and visible sign of an inward fear.

HASH: There is no definition for this word — nobody knows what hash is.

HEAVEN: A place where the wicked cease from troubling you with talk of their personal affairs, and the good listen with attention while you expound your own.

HISTORY: An account mostly false, of events mostly unimportant, which are brought about by rulers mostly knaves, and soldiers mostly fools.

HOSTILITY: A peculiarly sharp and specially applied sense of the earth's overpopulation.

HOVEL: The fruit of a flower called the palace.

HUSBAND: One who, having dined, is charged with the care of the plate.

IDIOT: A member of a large and powerful tribe whose influence in human affairs has always been dominant and controlling.

IGNORAMUS: A person unacquainted with certain kinds of knowledge familiar to yourself, and having certain other kinds that you know nothing about.

IMAGINATION: A warehouse of facts, with poet and liar in joint ownership.

IMMIGRANT: An unenlightened person who thinks one country better than another.

IMMORAL: Inexpedient.

IMPARTIAL: Unable to perceive any promise of personal advantage from espousing either side of a controversy or adopting either of two conflicting opinions.

IMPIETY: Your irreverence toward my deity.

IMPUNITY: Wealth.

INCOMPATIBILITY: In matrimony a similarity of tastes, particularly the taste for domination.

INK: A villainous compound of tannogallate of iron, gum-arabic and water, chiefly used to facilitate the infection of idiocy and promote intellectual crime.

INTERPRETER: One who enables persons of different languages to understand each other by repeating to each what it would have been to the interpreter's advantage for the other to have said.

INVENTOR: A person who makes an ingenious arrangement of wheels, levers and springs, and believes it civilization.

FUTURE: That period of time in which our affairs prosper, our friends are true and our happiness is assured.

JEALOUS: Unduly concerned about the preservation of that which can be lost only if not worth keeping.

JUSTICE: A commodity which is a more or less adulterated condition the State sells to the citizen as a reward for his allegiance, taxes and personal service.

KLEPTOMANIAC: A rich thief.

LAWYER: One skilled in circumvention of the law.

LITIGATION: A machine which you go into as a pig and come out of as a sausage.

LONGEVITY: Uncommon extension of the fear of death.

MAD: Affected with a high degree of intellectual independence.

MAGIC: An art of converting superstition into coin.

MARRIAGE: The state or condition of a community consisting of a master, a mistress and two slaves, making in all, two.

MIRACLE: An act or event out of the order of nature and unaccountable, as beating a normal hand of four kings and an ace with four aces and a king.

MORAL: Having the quality of general expediency.

MYTHOLOGY: The body of a primitive people's beliefs concerning its origin, early history, heroes, deities and so forth, as distinguished from the true accounts which it invents later.

NOVEL: A short story padded.

OBSERVATORY: A place where astronomers conjecture away the guesses of their predecessors.

OBSOLETE: No longer used by the timid.

OCEAN: A body of water occupying about two-thirds of a world made for man — who has no gills.

OPPORTUNITY: A favorable occasion for grasping a disappointment.

OPTIMIST: A proponent of the doctrine that black is white.

PATRIOT: One to whom the interests of a part seem superior to those of the whole. The dupe of statesmen and the tool of conquerors.

PERSEVERANCE: A lowly virtue whereby mediocrity achieves an inglorious success.

PESSIMISM: A philosophy forced upon the convictions of the observer by the disheartening prevalence of the optimist with his scarecrow hope and his unsightly smile.

PHILOSOPHY: A route of many roads leading from nowhere to nothing.

PICTURE: A representation in two dimensions of something wearisome in three.

PIRACY: Commerce without its folly-swaddles, just as God made it.

PLAGIARISM: A literary coincidence compounded of a discreditable priority and an honorable subsequence.

PLAN: To bother about the best method of accomplishing an accidental result.

POLITENESS: The most acceptable hypocrisy.

POLITICS: The conduct of public affairs for private advantage.

POSITIVE: Mistaken at the top of one's voice.

POVERTY: A file provided for the teeth of the rats of reform.

PRAY: To ask that the laws of the universe be annulled on behalf of a single petitioner confessedly unworthy.

PRECEDENT: In law, a previous decision, rule or practice which has whatever force and authority a judge may choose to give it, thereby greatly simplifying his task of doing as he pleases.

PREFERENCE: A sentiment, or frame of mind, induced by the erroneous belief that one thing is better than another.

PREJUDICE: A vagrant opinion without visible means of support.

PRESENT: That part of eternity dividing the domain of disappointment from the realm of hope.

PRESENTABLE: Hideously appareled after the manner of the time and place.

PRESIDENT: The leading figure in a small group of men of whom — and of whom only — it is positively known that immense numbers of their countrymen did not want any of them for President.

PRICE: Value, plus a reasonable sum for the wear and tear of conscience in demanding it.

PROOF: Evidence having a shade more of plausibility than of unlikelihood.

PHOTOGRAPH:
A picture painted
by the sun without
instruction in art.

ILLUSTRATIONS ©2008 STEVEN CERIO

QUOTATION: The act of repeating erroneously the words of another.

RADICALISM: The conservatism of tomorrow injected into the affairs of today.

RAILROAD: The chief of many mechanical devices enabling us to get away from where we are to where we are no better off.

REALISM: The art of depicting nature as it is seen by toads. The charm suffusing a landscape painted by a mole, or a story written by a measuring-worm.

REASON: To weigh probabilities in the scales of desire.

REASONABLE: Accessible to the infection of our own opinions.

REBEL: A proponent of a new misrule who has failed to establish it.

RECOLLECT: To recall with additions something not previously known.

RECONSIDER: To seek a justification for a decision already made.

RECOUNT: In American politics, another throw of the dice, accorded to the player against whom they are loaded.

REDEMPTION: Deliverance of sinners from the penalty of their sin, through their murder of the deity against whom they sinned.

RELIGION: A daughter of Hope and Fear, explaining to Ignorance the nature of the Unknowable.

RESOLUTE: Obstinate in a course that we approve.

RESPONSIBILITY: A detachable burden easily shifted to the shoulders of God, Fate, Fortune, Luck or one's neighbor.

RESTITUTION: The founding or endowing of universities and public libraries by gift or bequest.

REVERENCE: The spiritual attitude of a man to a god and a dog to a man.

REVOLUTION: In politics, an abrupt change in the form of misgovernment. Revolutions are usually accompanied by a considerable effusion of blood, but are accounted worth it — this appraisement being made by beneficiaries whose blood had not the mischance to be shed.

RICH: Holding in trust and subject to an accounting the property of the indolent, the incompetent, the unthrifty, the envious and the luckless.

SCRIPTURES: The sacred books of our holy religion, as distinguished from the false and profane writings on which all other faiths are based.

SENATE: A body of elderly gentlemen charged with high duties and misdemeanors.

TELEPHONE: An invention of the devil which abrogates some of the advantages of making a disagreeable person keep his distance.

TRIAL: A formal inquiry designed to prove and put upon record the blameless characters of judges, advocates and jurors. In order to effect this purpose it is necessary to supply a contrast in the person of one who is called the defendant, the prisoner, or the accused. If the contrast is made sufficiently clear this person is made to undergo such an affliction as will give the virtuous gentlemen a comfortable sense of their immunity, added to that of their worth.

TRUTH: An ingenious compound of desirability and appearance.

TRUST: A large corporation composed in greater part of thrifty working men, widows of small means, orphans in the care of guardians and the courts, with many similar malefactors and public enemies.

ULTIMATUM: In diplomacy, a last demand before resorting to concessions.

UNIVERSALIST: One who forgoes the advantage of a hell for persons of another faith.

VOTE: The instrument and symbol of a freeman's power to make a fool of himself and a wreck of his country.

WAR: A by-product of the arts of peace. The soil of peace is thickly sown with the seeds of war and singularly suited to their germination and growth.

WORMS'-MEAT: The finished product of which we are the raw material.

YEAR: A period of three hundred and sixty-five disappointments.

ZEAL: A certain nervous disorder afflicting the young and inexperienced.

The Hypnotist

a story by
AMBROSE BIERCE

illustrated by
MICHAEL SLACK

My first knowledge that I possessed unusual powers came to me in my fourteenth year, when at school. Happening one day to have forgotten to bring my luncheon, I gazed longingly at that of a small girl who was preparing to eat hers. Looking up, her eyes met mine and she seemed unable to withdraw them. After a moment of hesitancy she came forward in an absent kind of way and surrendered her little basket with its tempting contents and walked away.

After that I had not the trouble to bring a luncheon for myself: that little girl was my daily purveyor. The girl was always persuaded that she had eaten all herself; and later in the day her tearful complaints of hunger surprised the teacher, entertained the pupils, earned for her the sobriquet of Greedy-Gut and filled me with a peace past understanding.

A disagreeable feature of this otherwise satisfactory condition of things was the necessary secrecy. The plan that I finally adopted to free myself from the consequences of my own powers excited a wide and keen interest at the time, and that part of it which consisted in the death of the girl was severely condemned, but it is hardly pertinent to the scope of this narrative.

For some years afterward I had little opportunity to practice hypnotism; such small essays as I made at it were commonly barren of other recognition than solitary confinement on a bread-and-water diet. It was when I was about to leave the scene of these small disappointments that my one really important feat was performed.

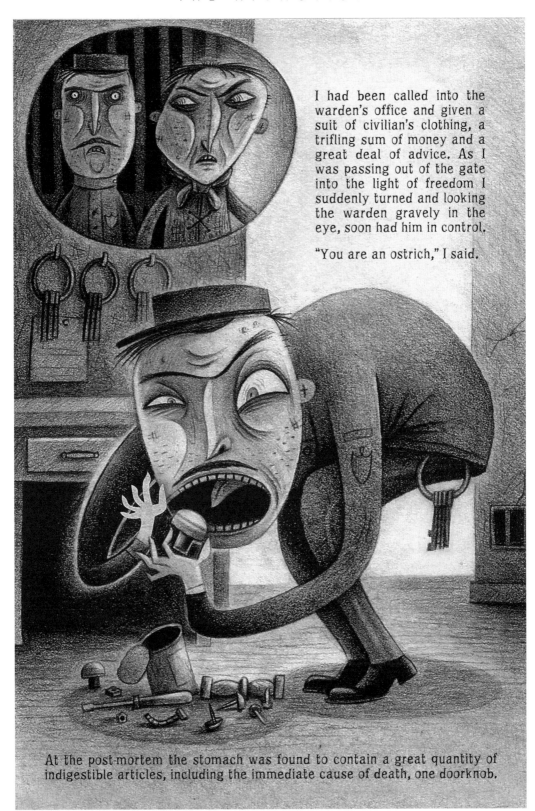

I had been called into the warden's office and given a suit of civilian's clothing, a trifling sum of money and a great deal of advice. As I was passing out of the gate into the light of freedom I suddenly turned and looking the warden gravely in the eye, soon had him in control.

"You are an ostrich," I said.

At the post-mortem the stomach was found to contain a great quantity of indigestible articles, including the immediate cause of death, one doorknob.

It was while going afoot to the home of my childhood that I found my parents. They were eating luncheon under an oak tree in the center of a field. The sight of the luncheon called up painful memories of my school days. Approaching the guilty couple, who at once recognized me, I ventured to suggest that I share their hospitality.

"There is sufficient for but two, my son," said the author of my being, with characteristic pomposity. "I am not, I hope, insensible to the hunger in your eyes, but —"

My father has never completed that sentence; what he mistook for hunger was simply the earnest gaze of the hypnotist. In a few seconds he was at my service. A few more sufficed for the lady, and the dictates of a just resentment could be carried into effect. "My former father," I said, "You and the lady here are, in truth, two broncos — wild stallions both, and unfriendly."

Scarcely had the words fallen from my lips when their flying legs crossed and mingled in combat, uttering their frenzy in the nameless sounds of the furious brutes which they believed themselves to be! The valor of my dear parents in the hour of danger can never cease to be to me a source of pride and gratification. At the end of it all two battered, tattered, bloody and fragmentary vestiges of mortality attested the solemn fact that the author of the strife was an orphan.

Arrested for provoking a breach of the peace, I was tried in the Court of Technicalities and Continuances whence, after fifteen years of proceedings, my attorney is moving to get the case taken to the Court of Remandment for New Trials.

Such are a few of my principal experiments in the mysterious force or agency known as hypnotic suggestion. Whether or not it could be employed by a bad man for an unworthy purpose I am unable to say.

BIERCE'S FABLES

a collection of short pieces by
AMBROSE BIERCE

adapted & illustrated by

SHARY FLENNIKEN

**ANTONELLA CAPUTO
& NICK MILLER**

MARK DANCEY

NEALE BLANDEN

JACKIE SMITH

DAN O'NEILL

GEORGE SELLAS

TODD LOVERING

DEVON DEVEREAUX

P.S. MUELLER

CHAD CARPENTER

EVERT GERADTS

ROGER LANGRIDGE

SIMON GANE

WILLIAM L. BROWN

ANTON EMDIN

LANCE TOOKS

LISA K. WEBER

JOHNNY RYAN

J.B. BONIVERT

ILLUSTRATION ©2003 STUDIO JAY-BEE

The Man Who Cried Wolf!

by Ambrose Bierce • illustrated by Shary Flenniken

A SHEPHERD OF A FACETIOUS TURN OF MIND ONCE CRIED: WOLF! WOLF! AND HIS NEIGHBORS, RUNNING TO ASSIST HIM AND FINDING NO WOLF, BEAT HIM CRUELLY FOR DECEIVING THEM.

SOON AFTERWARD, HIS FLOCK WAS ATTACKED BY A LION AND THE SHEPHERD CRIED OUT: WOLF! WOLF! AS BEFORE.

THE NEIGHBORS SAID: THAT RASCAL IS TRYING TO FOOL US AGAIN, AND WE WILL CUDGEL HIM AS BEFORE.

BUT WHEN THEY HAD COME TO THE SPOT, THE LION ATE THEM AND THE HUMOROUS SHEPHERD WAS GREATLY PLEASED WITH THE SUCCESS OF HIS STRATAGEM.

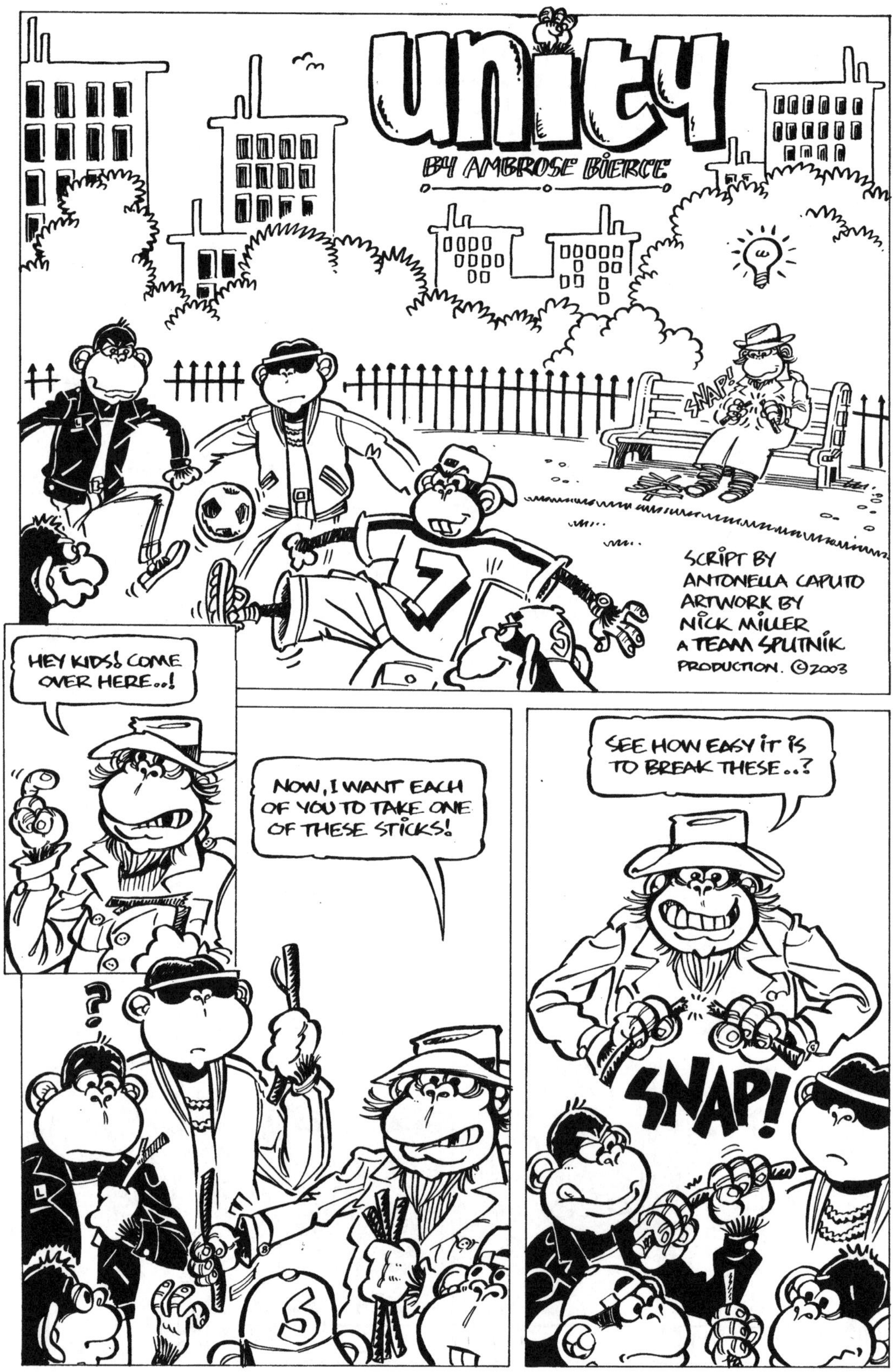
UNITY
BY AMBROSE BIERCE
SNAP!
SCRIPT BY ANTONELLA CAPUTO ARTWORK BY NICK MILLER A TEAM SPUTNIK PRODUCTION. ©2003
HEY KIDS! COME OVER HERE..!
NOW, I WANT EACH OF YOU TO TAKE ONE OF THESE STICKS!
?
SEE HOW EASY IT IS TO BREAK THESE..?
SNAP!

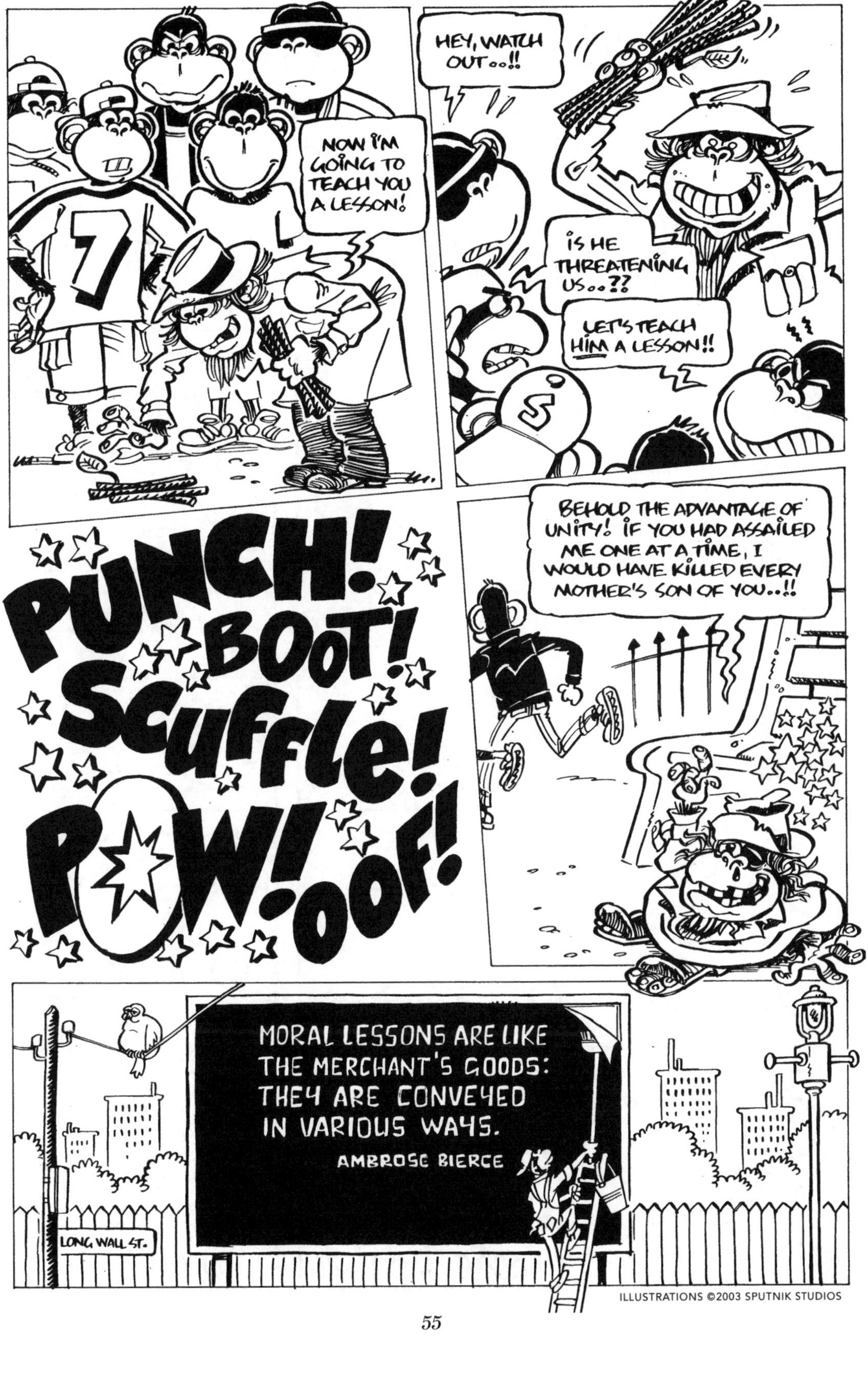
NOW I'M GOING TO TEACH YOU A LESSON!
7
HEY, WATCH OUT..!!
IS HE THREATENING US..??
LET'S TEACH HIM A LESSON!!
S
PUNCH! BOOT! SCUFFLE! POW! OOF!
BEHOLD THE ADVANTAGE OF UNITY! IF YOU HAD ASSAILED ME ONE AT A TIME, I WOULD HAVE KILLED EVERY MOTHER'S SON OF YOU..!!
MORAL LESSONS ARE LIKE THE MERCHANT'S GOODS: THEY ARE CONVEYED IN VARIOUS WAYS.
AMBROSE BIERCE
LONG WALL ST.

COMPROMISE WITH A CAMEL

Story by **Ambrose Bierce** • Illustrated by **Mark Dancey**

Moral:
A compromise is not always a settlement satisfactory to both parties.

ILLUSTRATIONS ©2003 MARK DANCEY

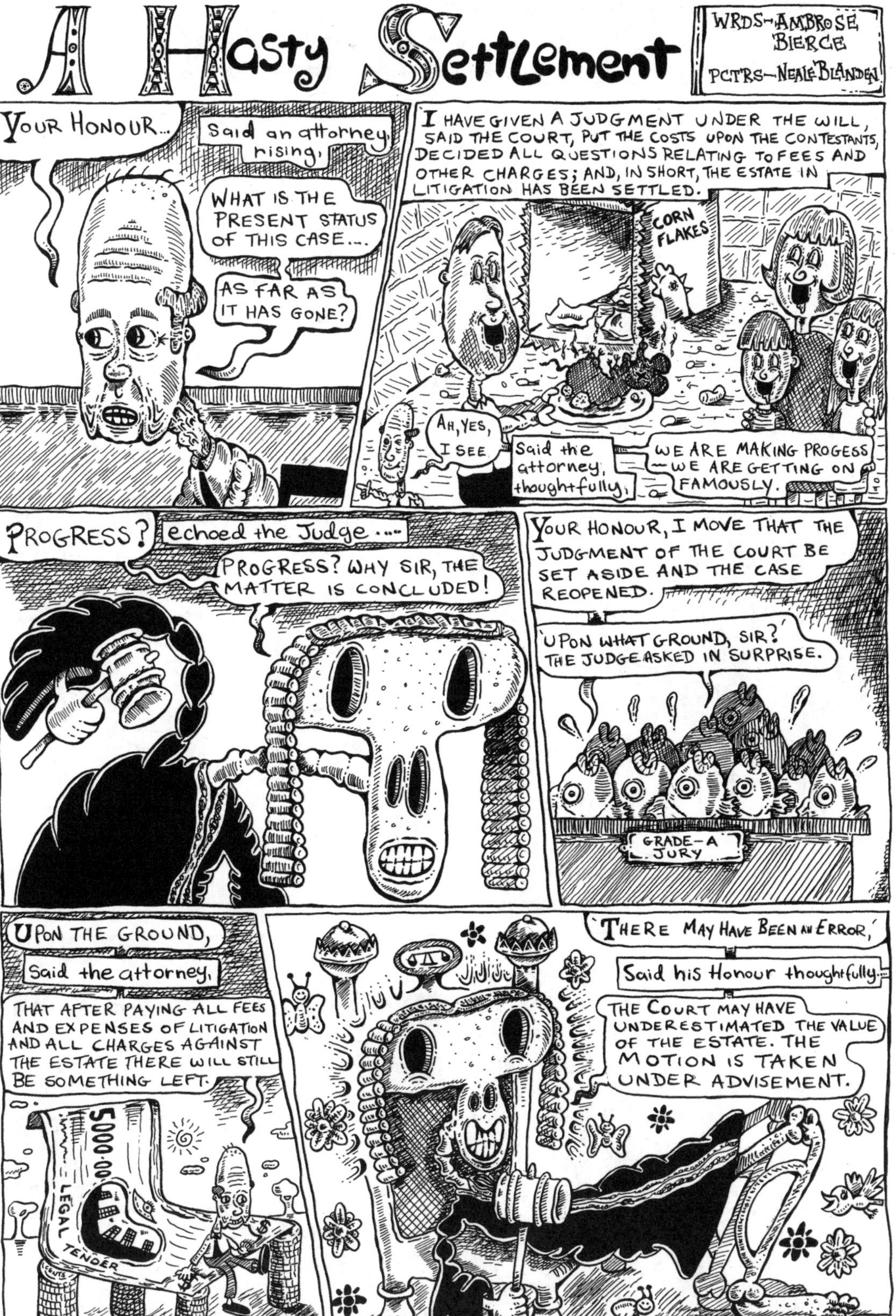
A Hasty Settlement
WRDS–AMBROSE BIERCE
PCT'RS–NEALE BLANDEN
YOUR HONOUR...
Said an attorney, rising,
WHAT IS THE PRESENT STATUS OF THIS CASE...
AS FAR AS IT HAS GONE?
I HAVE GIVEN A JUDGMENT UNDER THE WILL, SAID THE COURT, PUT THE COSTS UPON THE CONTESTANTS, DECIDED ALL QUESTIONS RELATING TO FEES AND OTHER CHARGES; AND, IN SHORT, THE ESTATE IN LITIGATION HAS BEEN SETTLED.
CORN FLAKES
AH, YES, I SEE.
Said the attorney, thoughtfully,
WE ARE MAKING PROGESS —WE ARE GETTING ON FAMOUSLY.
PROGRESS?
echoed the Judge....
PROGRESS? WHY SIR, THE MATTER IS CONCLUDED!
YOUR HONOUR, I MOVE THAT THE JUDGMENT OF THE COURT BE SET ASIDE AND THE CASE REOPENED.
'UPON WHAT GROUND, SIR?' THE JUDGE ASKED IN SURPRISE.
GRADE–A JURY
UPON THE GROUND,
Said the attorney,
THAT AFTER PAYING ALL FEES AND EXPENSES OF LITIGATION AND ALL CHARGES AGAINST THE ESTATE THERE WILL STILL BE SOMETHING LEFT.
5000.00
LEGAL TENDER
'THERE MAY HAVE BEEN AN ERROR,'
Said his Honour thoughtfully....
THE COURT MAY HAVE UNDERESTIMATED THE VALUE OF THE ESTATE. THE MOTION IS TAKEN UNDER ADVISEMENT.
NB 11.02

Professional Courtesy

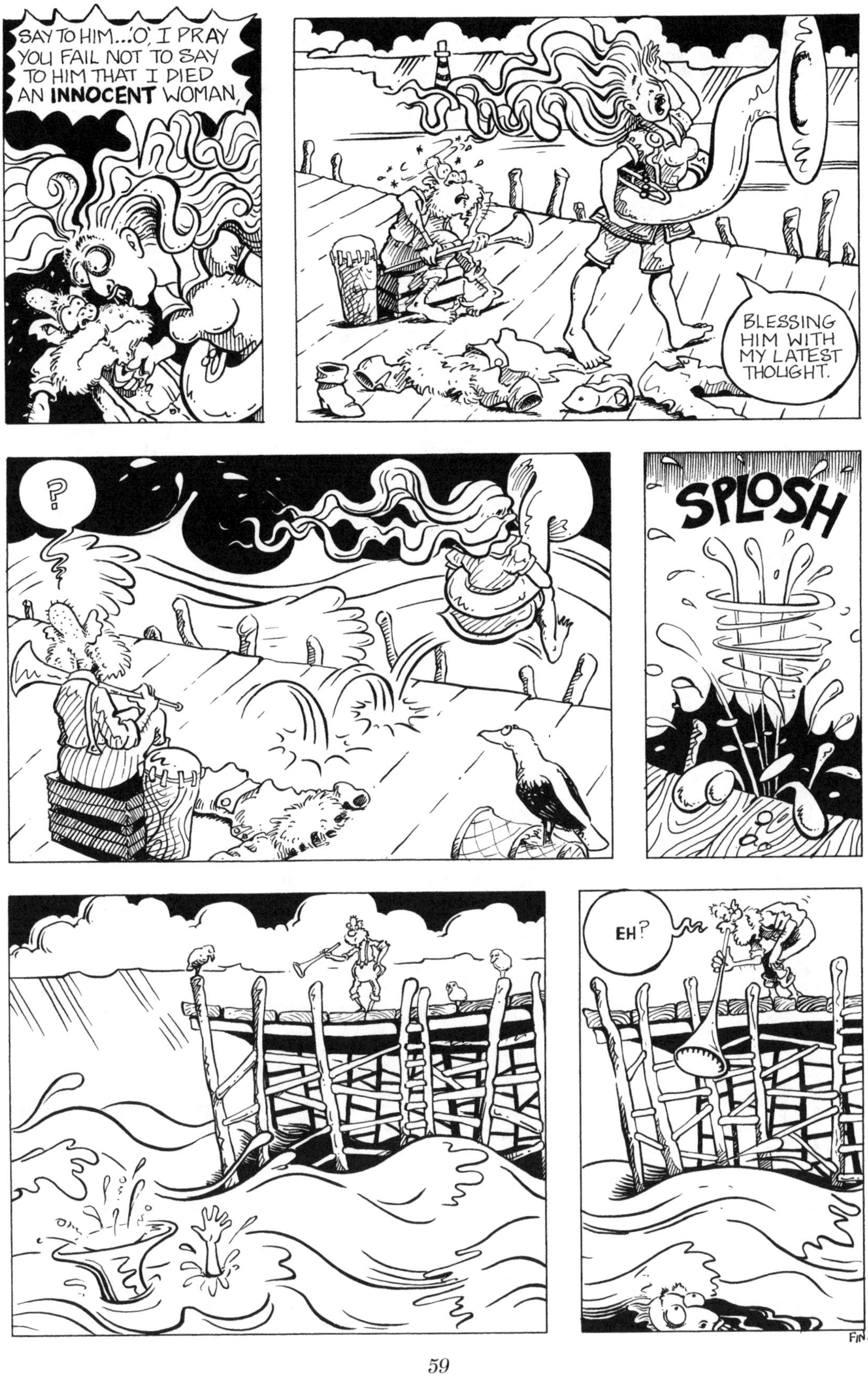
SAY TO HIM...'O', I PRAY YOU FAIL NOT TO SAY TO HIM THAT I DIED AN **INNOCENT** WOMAN,'
BLESSING HIM WITH MY LATEST THOUGHT.
?
SPLOSH
EH?
FIN.

ILLUSTRATIONS ©2003 JACKIE SMITH

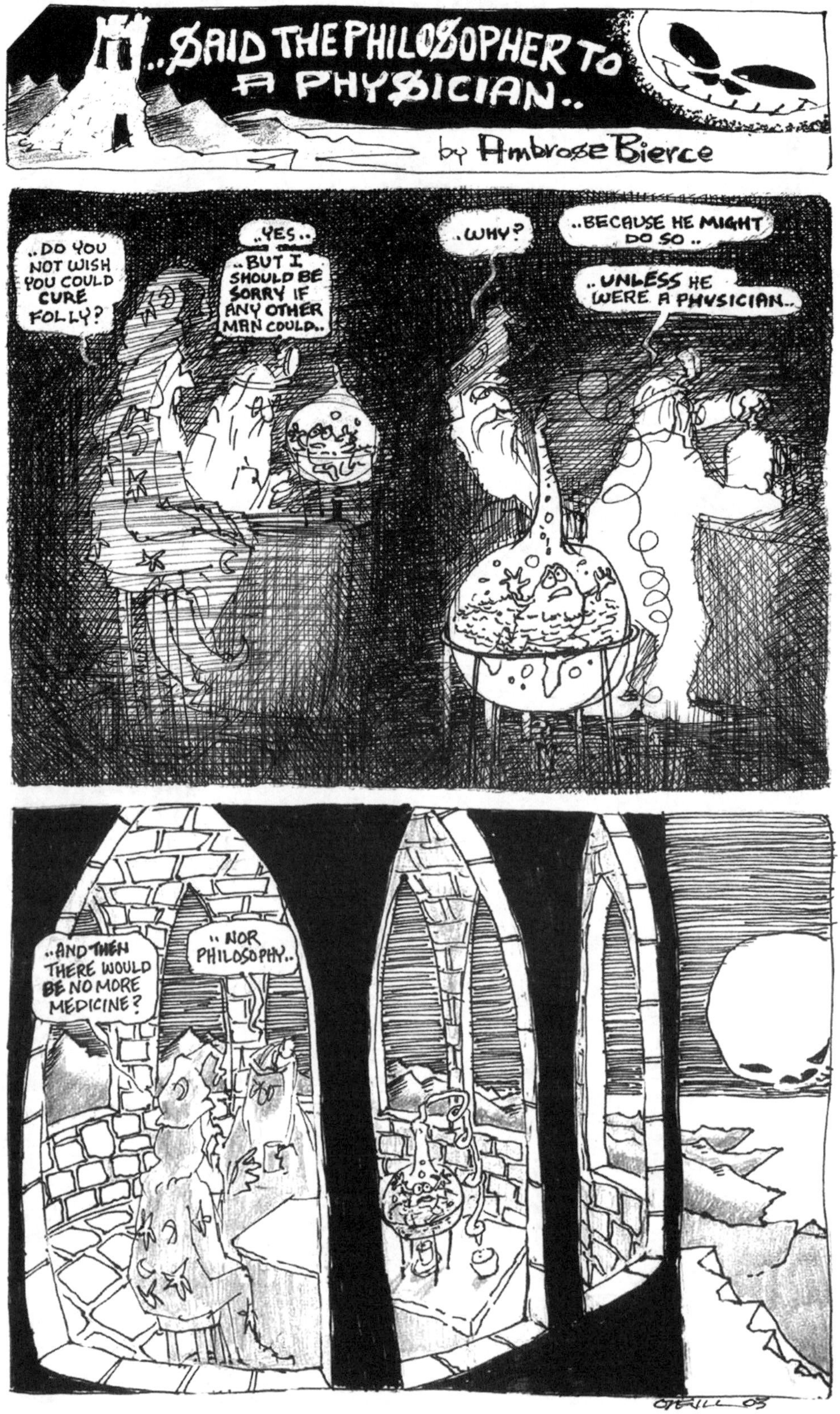
..SAID THE PHILOSOPHER TO A PHYSICIAN..
by Ambrose Bierce
..DO YOU NOT WISH YOU COULD CURE FOLLY?
..YES..
..BUT I SHOULD BE SORRY IF ANY OTHER MAN COULD..
..WHY?
..BECAUSE HE MIGHT DO SO..
..UNLESS HE WERE A PHYSICIAN..
..AND THEN THERE WOULD BE NO MORE MEDICINE?
..NOR PHILOSOPHY..

The Disinterested Arbiter

by Ambrose Bierce
Illustrated by George Sellas

Two dogs who had been fighting for a bone,
without advantage to either,
referred their dispute to a sheep.

The sheep patiently heard their
statements, then flung the
bone into a pond.

"Why did you do that?" cried the dogs.

"Because," replied the sheep,
"I am a vegetarian."

THE HARE AND THE TORTOISE

A hare, having ridiculed the slow tortoise, was challenged by the latter to run a race, with a fox to be the judge. They got off well, the hare at the top of her speed, the tortoise plodding leisurely. After some time he discovered the hare by the wayside, apparently asleep, and seeing a chance to win pushed on as fast as he could, arriving at the goal hours afterward, exhausted and claiming victory. "Not so," said the fox, "the hare was here long ago, and went back to cheer you on your way."

THE TORTOISE AND THE HARE

Of two writers, one was brilliant but indolent; the other though dull, industrious. They set out for the goal of fame with equal opportunities. Before they died, the brilliant one was detected in seventy languages as the author of but two or three books of fiction and poetry, while the other was honoured in the Bureau of Statistics of his native land as the compiler of sixteen volumes of tabulated information relating to the domestic hog.

illustration by Todd Lovering

THE TAIL OF THE SPHINX

story by **AMBROSE BIERCE**
illustrated by **DEVON DEVEREAUX**

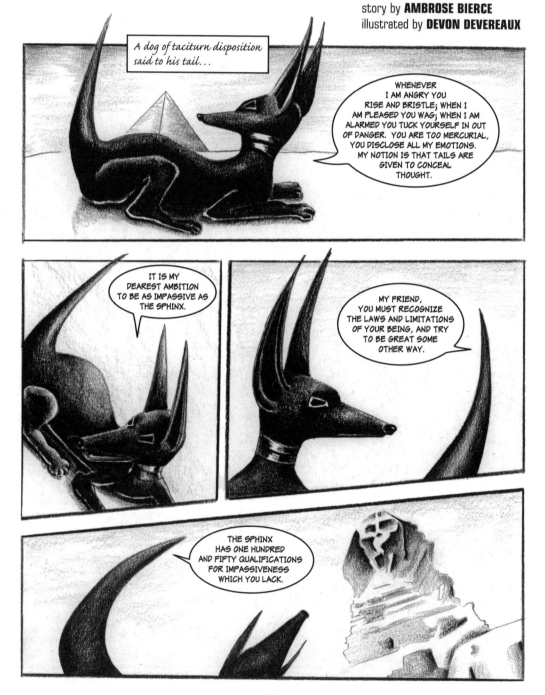

A dog of taciturn disposition said to his tail...

WHENEVER I AM ANGRY YOU RISE AND BRISTLE; WHEN I AM PLEASED YOU WAG; WHEN I AM ALARMED YOU TUCK YOURSELF IN OUT OF DANGER. YOU ARE TOO MERCURIAL, YOU DISCLOSE ALL MY EMOTIONS. MY NOTION IS THAT TAILS ARE GIVEN TO CONCEAL THOUGHT.

IT IS MY DEAREST AMBITION TO BE AS IMPASSIVE AS THE SPHINX.

MY FRIEND, YOU MUST RECOGNIZE THE LAWS AND LIMITATIONS OF YOUR BEING, AND TRY TO BE GREAT SOME OTHER WAY.

THE SPHINX HAS ONE HUNDRED AND FIFTY QUALIFICATIONS FOR IMPASSIVENESS WHICH YOU LACK.

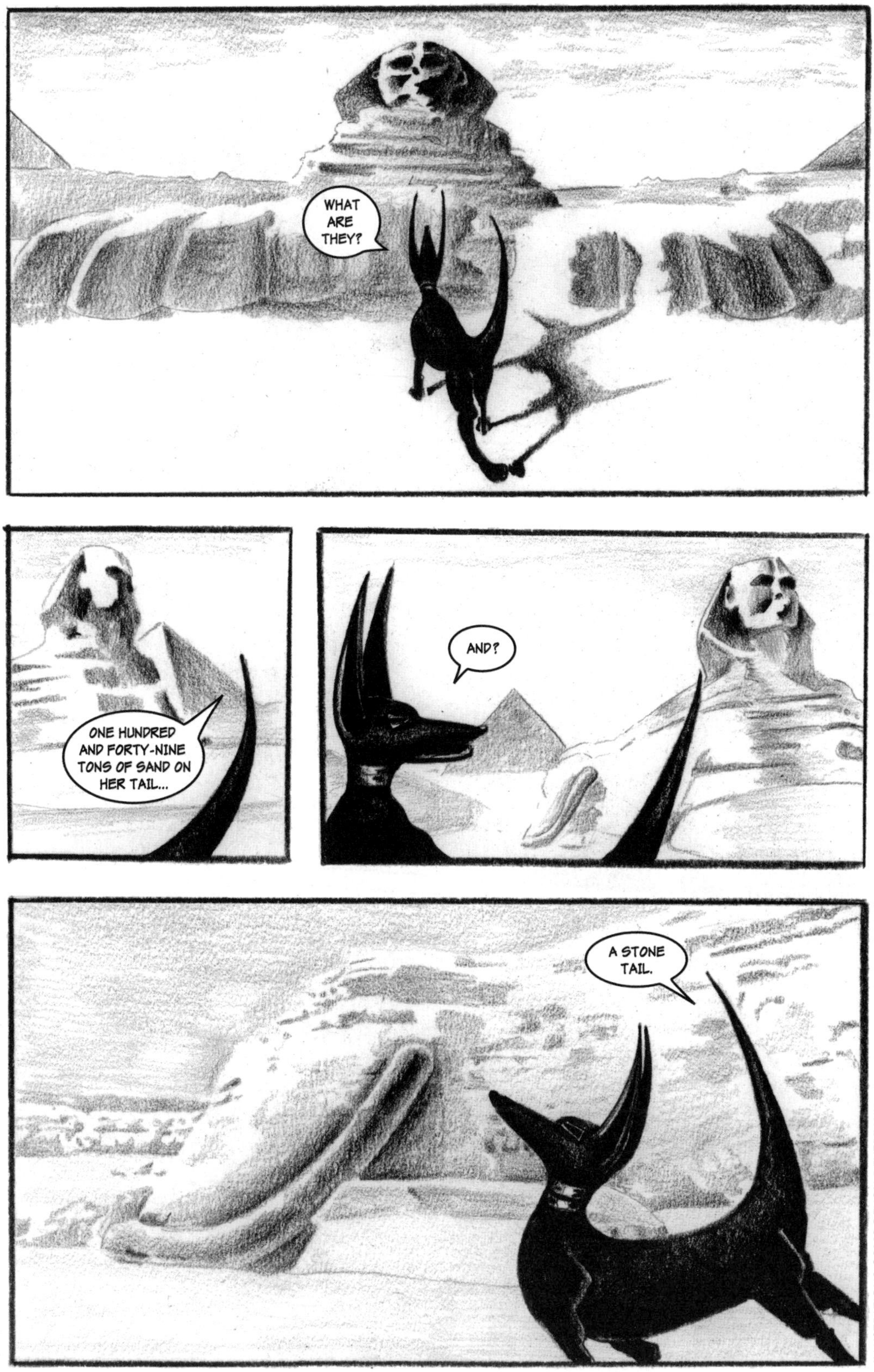
WHAT ARE THEY?
ONE HUNDRED AND FORTY-NINE TONS OF SAND ON HER TAIL...
AND?
A STONE TAIL.

The Deceased and His Heirs

illustrated by **P.S. MUELLER**

A man died leaving a large estate and many sorrowful relations who claimed it. After some years, when all but one had had judgment given against them, that one was awarded the estate, which he asked his attorney to have appraised.

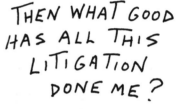

THERE IS NOTHING LEFT TO APPRAISE.

THEN WHAT GOOD HAS ALL THIS LITIGATION DONE ME?

YOU HAVE BEEN A GOOD CLIENT TO ME, BUT I MUST SAY YOU BETRAY A SURPRISING IGNORANCE OF THE PURPOSE OF LITIGATION.

P.S. MUELLER

DOCILITY'S REWARD by AMBROSE BIERCE

illustrated by Chad Carpenter

The moral of this story isn't what you think it is. It is this: The chops of another man's mutton are always nice eating.

THE SPIDER AND THE FLY

"Pray walk into my parlour," said the spider to the fly.

"That is not quite original," the latter made reply.

"If that's the way you plagiarize, your fame will be a fib!

But I'll walk into your parlour, while I pitch into your crib.

But before I cross your threshold, sir, if I may make so free,

Pray let me introduce to you my friend, the wicked flea."

"How do you?" says the spider, as his welcome he extends;

"How doth the busy little bee, and all our other friends?"

"Quite well, I think, and quite unchanged," the flea said; "though I learn,

In certain quarters well-informed, 'tis feared the worm will turn."

"Humph!" said the fly; "I do not understand this talk, not I!"

"It is classical allusion," said the spider to the fly.

art by Evert Geradts

The Child's Provider

by AMBROSE BIERCE

Adaptation by Roger Langridge

MR. GOBOFFLE HAD A SMALL CHILD, NO WIFE, A LARGE DOG, AND A HOUSE.

AS HE WAS UNABLE TO AFFORD THE EXPENSE OF A NURSE, HE WAS ACCUSTOMED TO LEAVE THE CHILD IN THE CARE OF THE DOG, WHO WAS MUCH ATTACHED TO IT, WHILE ABSENT AT A DISTANT RESTAURANT FOR HIS MEALS...

...TAKING THE PRECAUTION TO LOCK THEM UP TOGETHER TO PREVENT KIDNAPPING.

ONE DAY, WHILE AT HIS DINNER, HE CROWDED A LARGE, HARD-BOILED POTATO DOWN HIS NECK...

...AND IT CONDUCTED HIM INTO ETERNITY.

HIS CLAY WAS TAKEN TO THE CORONER'S, AND THE GREAT WORLD WENT ON, MARRYING AND GIVING IN MARRIAGE, LYING, CHEATING, AND PRAYING, AS IF HE HAD NEVER EXISTED.

MEANTIME THE DOG HAD, AFTER SEVERAL DAYS OF NEGLECT, FORCED AN EGRESS THROUGH A WINDOW...

... AND A NEIGHBORING BAKER RECEIVED A CALL FROM HIM DAILY.

WALKING GRAVELY IN, HE WOULD DEPOSIT A PIECE OF SILVER...

... AND RECEIVING A ROLL AND HIS CHANGE WOULD MARCH OFF HOMEWARD.

AS THIS WAS A RATHER UNUSUAL PROCEEDING IN A CUR OF HIS SPECIES, THE BAKER ONE DAY FOLLOWED HIM...

... AND AS THE DOG LEAPED JOYOUSLY INTO THE WINDOW OF THE DESERTED HOUSE...

... THE MAN OF DOUGH APPROACHED AND LOOKED IN.

WHAT WAS HIS SURPRISE TO SEE THE DOG DEPOSIT HIS BREAD CALMLY UPON THE FLOOR...

... AND FALL TO TENDERLY LICKING THE FACE OF A BEAUTIFUL CHILD!

IT IS BUT FAIR TO EXPLAIN THAT THERE WAS NOTHING BUT THE FACE REMAINING.

BUT THIS DOG DID SO LOVE THE CHILD!

The Policeman and the Citizen

By Ambrose Bierce
Illustrated by Simon Gane

A policeman, finding a man that had fallen in a fit, said, "This man is drunk," and began beating him on the head with his club.

A passing citizen said: "Why do you murder a man that is already harmless?"

Thereupon the policeman left the man in a fit and attacked the citizen, who, after receiving several severe contusions, ran away.

"Alas," said the policeman, "why did I not attack the sober one before exhausting myself upon the other?"

Thenceforward he pursued that plan, and by zeal and diligence rose to be Chief, and sobriety is unknown in the region subject to his sway.

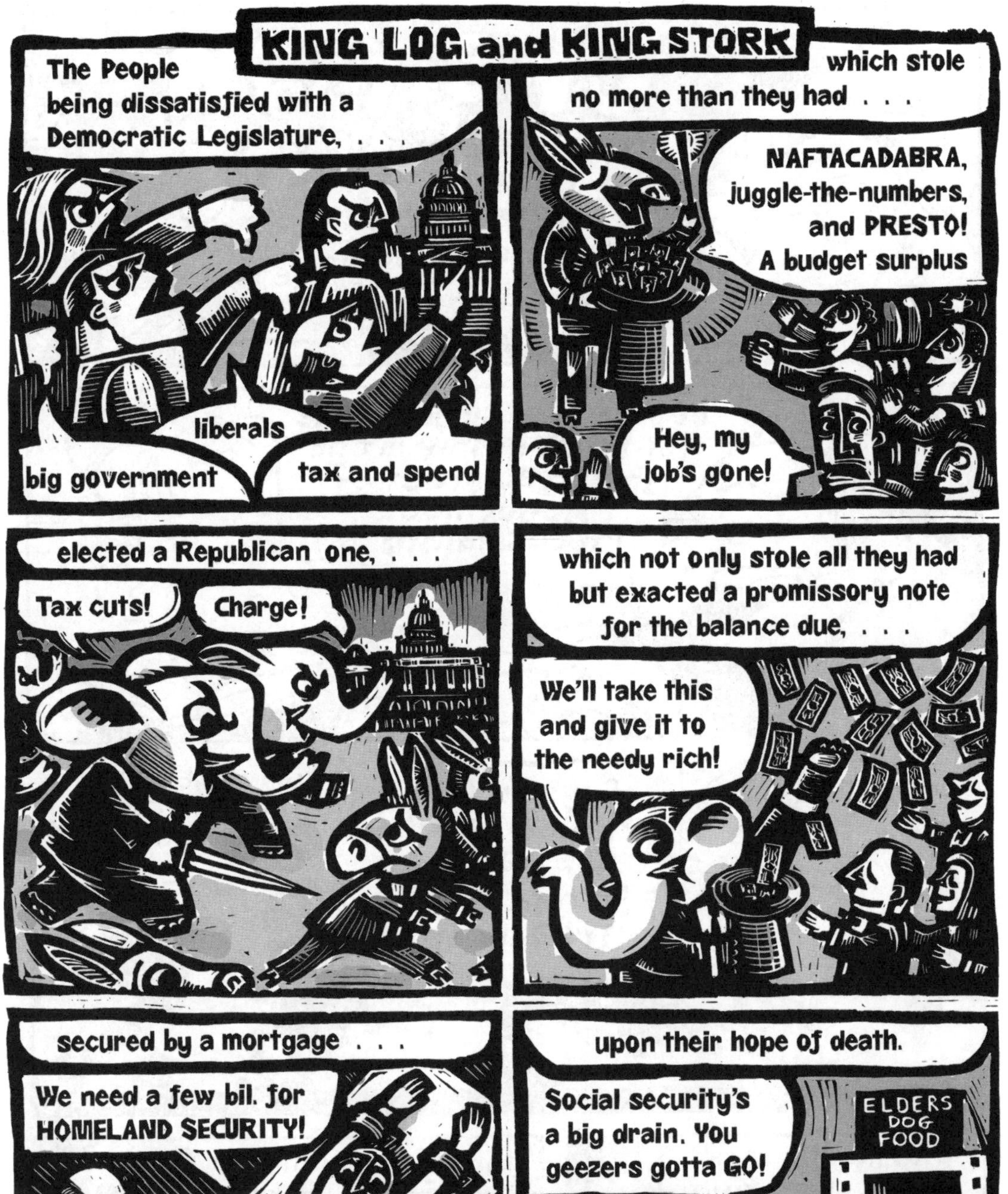
KING LOG and KING STORK
The People being dissatisfied with a Democratic Legislature, . . .
liberals
big government
tax and spend
which stole no more than they had . . .
NAFTACADABRA, juggle-the-numbers, and PRESTO! A budget surplus
Hey, my job's gone!
elected a Republican one, . . .
Tax cuts!
Charge!
which not only stole all they had but exacted a promissory note for the balance due, . . .
We'll take this and give it to the needy rich!
secured by a mortgage . . .
We need a few bil. for HOMELAND SECURITY!
MORTGAGE
Sign on the dotted tax-payer!
And a few hundred bil. for WAR
upon their hope of death.
Social security's a big drain. You geezers gotta GO!
ELDERS DOG FOOD
It's for HOMELAND SECURITY, Pops!
WM. L. BROWN 03

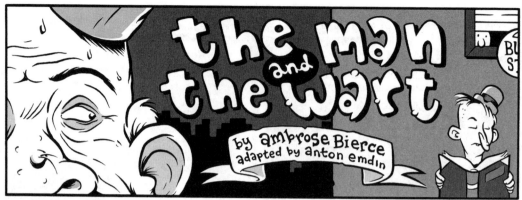

the man and the wart

by ambrose Bierce
adapted by anton emdin

Let me propose your name for membership in the Imperial Order of Abnormal Proboscidians...

...of which I am the High Noble Toby and Surreptitious Treasurer

two months ago I was the only member

one month ago there were two

today we number four Emperors of the Abnormal Proboscis in good standing ~ you know how that piles up

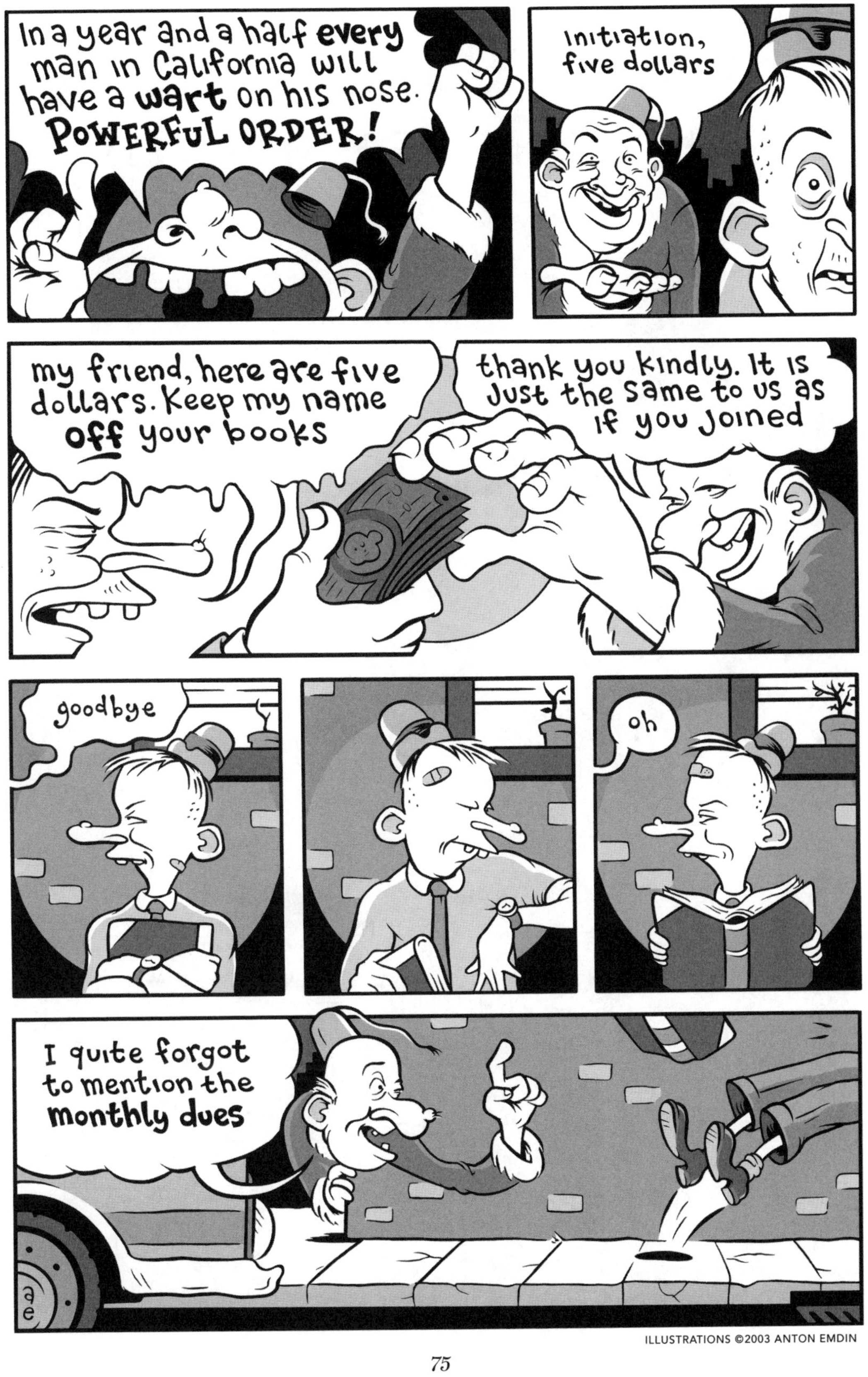
In a year and a half every man in California will have a wart on his nose. POWERFUL ORDER!
Initiation, five dollars
my friend, here are five dollars. Keep my name off your books
thank you kindly. It is just the same to us as if you joined
goodbye
oh
I quite forgot to mention the monthly dues
ae

THE SECRET OF HAPPINESS

HAVING BEEN TOLD BY AN ANGEL THAT
NOUREDDIN BECAR WAS THE HAPPIEST MAN
IN THE WORLD, THE SULTAN
CAUSED HIM TO BE BROUGHT
TO THE PALACE AND SAID:

"IMPART TO ME,
I COMMAND THEE,
THE SECRET OF THY
HAPPINESS."

BIERCE & TOOKS

"O FATHER OF THE SUN AND THE MOON," ANSWERED NOUREDDIN BECAR, "I DID NOT KNOW THAT I WAS HAPPY."

"THAT," SAID THE SULTAN, "IS THE SECRET THAT I SOUGHT."

NOUREDDIN BECAR RETIRED IN DEEP DEJECTION, FEARING THAT HIS NEW-FOUND HAPPINESS MIGHT FORSAKE HIM.

A DEATHBED REPENTANCE
illustrated by Lisa K. Weber

AN OLD MAN of seventy-five years lay dying. For a lifetime he had turned a deaf ear to religion, and steeped his soul in every current crime. He had robbed the orphan and plundered the widow; he had wrested from the hard hands of honest toil the rewards of labour; had lost at the gaming-table the wealth with which he should have endowed churches and Sunday schools; had wasted in riotous living the substance of his patrimony, and left his wife and children without bread. The intoxicating bowl had been his god — his belly had absorbed his entire attention. In carnal pleasures passed his days and nights, and to the maddening desires of his heart he had ministered without shame and without remorse. He was a bad, bad egg! And now this hardened iniquitor was to meet his Maker! Feebly and hesitatingly his breath fluttered upon his pallid lips. Weakly trembled the pulse in his flattened veins! Wife, children, mother-in-law, friends, who should have hovered lovingly about his couch, cheering his last moments and giving him medicine, he had killed with grief, or driven widely away; and he was now dying alone by the inadequate light of a tallow candle, deserted by heaven and by earth. No, not by heaven. Suddenly the door was pushed softly open, and there entered the good minister, whose pious counsel the suffering wretch had in health so often derided. Solemnly the man of God advanced, Bible in hand. Long and silently he stood uncovered in the presence of death. Then with cold and impressive dignity he remarked, *"Miserable old sinner!"*

Old Jonas Lashworthy looked up. He sat up. The voice of that holy man put strength into his aged limbs, and he stood up. He was reserved for a better fate than to die like a neglected dog: Mr. Lashworthy was hanged for braining a minister of the Gospel with a boot-jack.

This touching tale has a moral:
In snatching a brand from the eternal burning, make sure of its condition, and be careful how you lay hold of it.

A Dog's Bequest

A DOG WHOSE SANDS OF LIFE WERE NEARLY RUN OUT LAY HELPLESS AT HIS MASTER'S DOOR.

BY GOOD OL' AMBROSE BIERCE

"ALAS!" HE WHINED, "AGE HAS ROBBED ME OF THE POWER TO FULFILL THE PURPOSE OF MY BEING AND THE FUNCTIONS OF MY RACE."

SNIF!

"MY VOICE IS SO IMPAIRED AND MY TEETH ARE SO INFREQUENT THAT I CAN NO LONGER ADEQUATELY TERRIFY THE INCAUTIOUS PASSER-BY..."

UH... BARK?

"...NOR PROPERLY MANGLE THE HARDY VISITOR."

KILL HETEROS

"THANK HEAVEN," HE ADDED REVERENTLY, "THE OLDER I GROW THE MORE OFFENSIVE I AM TO THE EYE AND NOSE, AND THE MORE I SCATTER PLENTY OF FLEAS O'ER A SMILING LAND."

JOHNNYR.COM

DAME FORTUNE AND THE TRAVELER
By Ambrose Bierce
Adapted by JB Bonivert

A WEARY TRAVELER WHO HAD LAIN DOWN AND FALLEN ASLEEP ON THE BRINK OF A DEEP WELL WAS DISCOVERED BY DAME FORTUNE...

OIL of DOG

Written by Ambrose Bierce
Illustrated by AnnIE OwEns

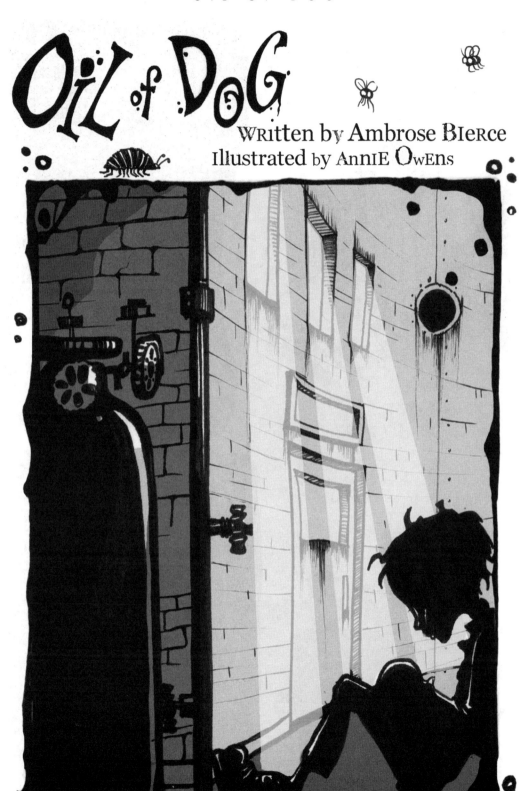

My name is Boffer Bings. I was born of honest parents in one of the humbler walks of life, my father being a manufacturer of dog oil and my mother having a small studio in the shadow of the village church, where she disposed of unwelcome babes.

In my boyhood I assisted my father in procuring dogs for his vats, and was frequently employed by my mother to carry away the debris of her work.

The law officers of the vicinity were opposed to my mother's business. The matter had never been made a political issue; it just happened so.

My father's business of making dog oil was, naturally, less unpopular. He had, as silent partners, all the physicians of the town, who seldom wrote a prescription which did not contain what they were pleased to designate as "Ol. can."

It is really the most valuable medicine ever discovered. But most persons are unwilling to make personal sacrifices for the afflicted.

Many of the fattest dogs in town had been forbidden to play with me — a fact which pained my young sensibilities. Looking back upon those days, I cannot but regret, at times, that by indirectly bringing my beloved parents to their death I was the author of misfortunes profoundly affecting my future.

One evening while passing my father's oil factory with the body of a foundling from my mother's studio I saw a constable who seemed to be closely watching my movements.

Young as I was, I had learned that a constable's acts, of whatever apparent character, are prompted by the most reprehensible motives.

I avoided him by dodging into the oilery by a side door which happened to stand ajar.

I locked it at once and was alone with my dead.

My father had retired for the night. The only light came from the furnace, which glowed a deep, rich crimson under one of the vats. Within the cauldron the oil rolled in indolent ebullition, occasionally pushing to the surface a piece of dog.

Seating myself to wait for the constable to go away, I held the body of the foundling in my lap. Ah, how beautiful it was.

I almost wished that the wound upon its breast, the work of my mother, had not been mortal.

It had been my custom to throw the babes into the river which nature had thoughtfully provided, but that night I did not dare to leave the oilery for fear of the constable.

"After all," I said to myself, "My father will never know the bones from those of a puppy. What difference can it make in the oil?"

In short, I took the first step in crime and brought myself untold sorrow by casting the babe into the cauldron.

The next day my father informed me and my mother that he had obtained the finest quality of oil that was ever seen. I deemed it my duty to explain, though palsied would have been my tongue if I could have foreseen the consequences. Finding a double profit in her business, my mother now devoted herself to it with a new assiduity.

She removed not only superfluous babes, but began gathering in children of a larger growth and even such adults as she could entice to the oilery.

My father, too, purveyed for his vats with diligence and zeal. The conversion of their neighbors into dog oil became the one passion of their lives.

An overwhelming greed took possession of their souls.

So enterprising had they now become that a public meeting was held and resolutions passed severely censuring them. It was intimated by the chairman that any further raids upon the population would be met in a spirit of hostility.

My parents left the meeting broken-hearted, and, I believe, not altogether sane. Anyhow, I deemed it prudent not to enter the oilery with them that night, but slept outside in a stable.

At about midnight some impulse caused me to rise and peer through a window into the furnace room, where my father now slept.

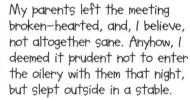

My father was not in bed; he had risen in his night clothes and was preparing a noose in a strong cord. From the looks which he cast at the door of my mother's bedroom I knew too well the purpose that he had in mind.

Suddenly the door of my mother's apartment was opened, noiselessly, and the two confronted each other. She also was in her night clothes, and held in her hand the tool of her trade.

She, too, had been unable to deny herself the last profit which the unfriendly action of the citizens and my absence had left her.

For one instant they looked into each other's blazing eyes and then sprang together with indescribable fury. Round and round the room they struggled, the man cursing, the woman shrieking, both fighting like demons — she to strike him with the dagger, he to strangle her with his bare hands. I know not how long I had the unhappiness to observe this disagreeable instance of domestic infelicity, but at last the combatants suddenly moved apart.

My father's breast and my mother's weapon showed evidences of contact. For another instant they glared at each other in the most unamiable way; then my poor father, feeling the hand of death upon him, leaped forward, grasped my dear mother in his arms, dragged her to the side of the boiling cauldron, collected all his failing energies, and sprang in with her! In a moment, both were adding their oil to that of the committee of citizens who had called the day before with an invitation to the public meeting.

Convinced that these unhappy events closed to me every avenue to an honorable career in that town, I removed to the famous city of Otumwee, where these memoirs are written with a heart full of remorse for a heedless act entailing so dismal a commercial disaster.

ILLUSTRATIONS ©2003 ANNIE OWENS

Curried COW

Story by
AMBROSE BIERCE

Adaptation by
MILTON KNIGHT

MY AUNT PATIENCE HAD A FAVORITE COW NAMED PHOEBE, WHO WAS NOT A GOOD COW, NOR A PROFITABLE ONE; FOR INSTEAD OF SECRETING MILK OR PRODUCING VEAL---

---PHOEBE CONCENTRATED ALL HER FACULTIES ON THE STUDY OF KICKING---

CURRYING COWS IS NOT, I THINK, A COMMON PRACTICE, EVEN IN MICHIGAN---

currycomb; a comb with teeth or ridges, for rubbing down or cleaning a horse's coat.

ANYHOW, MY AUNT ALWAYS MADE IT A CONDITION TO THE EMPLOYMENT OF A FARM SERVANT THAT HE SHOULD CURRY THE COW EVERY MORNING---

---HE WOULD ALWAYS GIVE NOTICE OF AN INTENTION TO QUIT---

BUT AFTER JUST ENOUGH TRIALS TO CONVINCE HIM THAT IT WAS NOT JUST A SUDDEN SPASM---

I DON'T KNOW HOW MANY MEN WERE REMOVED FROM MY AUNT'S EMPLOY IN THIS WAY---

BUT I SHOULD SAY A GREAT MANY.

AND IT WAS REMARKED THAT THE COW HAD 'KICKED THE FARM TO PIECES', IMPLYING THAT THE LAND WAS NOT PROPERLY CULTIVATED---

farm hand WANTED

HUSBAND WANTED

THERE BEING BUT **ONE** ELIGIBLE MALE IN ALL THAT COUNTY, AUNT PATIENCE SET HER HEART UPON *HIM*--

HE TURNED OUT TO BE A METHODIST, PARSON, NAMED *huggins*-

now, huggy dear, I'LL TELL YOU WHAT THERE IS TO DO ABOUT THE PLACE. FIRST, YOU MUST REPAIR ALL THE FENCES, EXTERMINATE THE CANADIAN THISTLES--

ASIDE FROM HIS UNCONSCIONABLE LENGTH, THE REV. BEROSUS HUGGINS WAS NOT SO BAD A FELLOW, AND NOBODY'S FOOL---

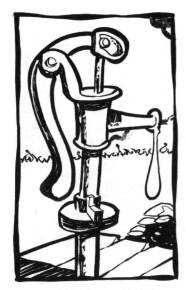

MINUTES LATER.

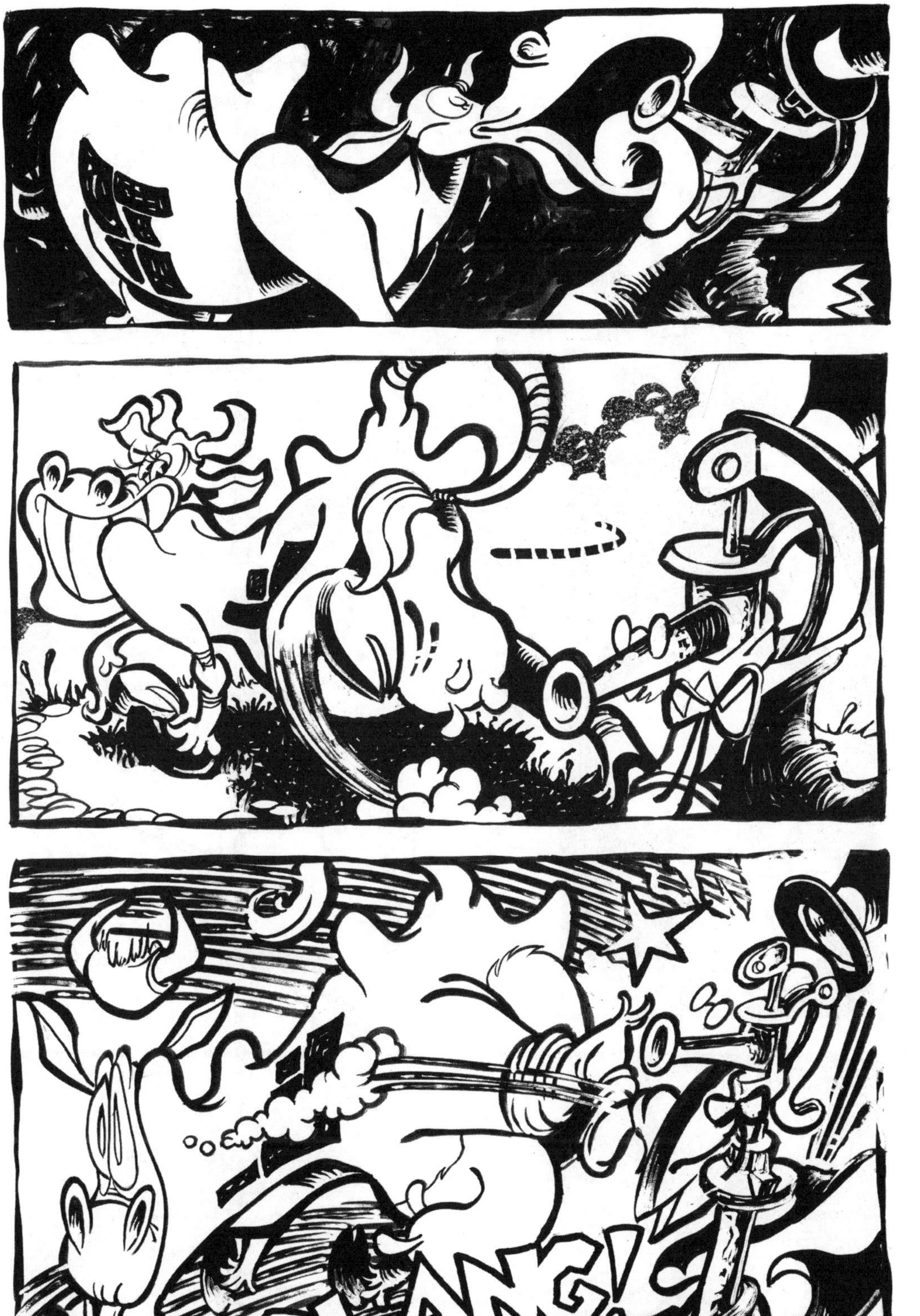
CLANG!

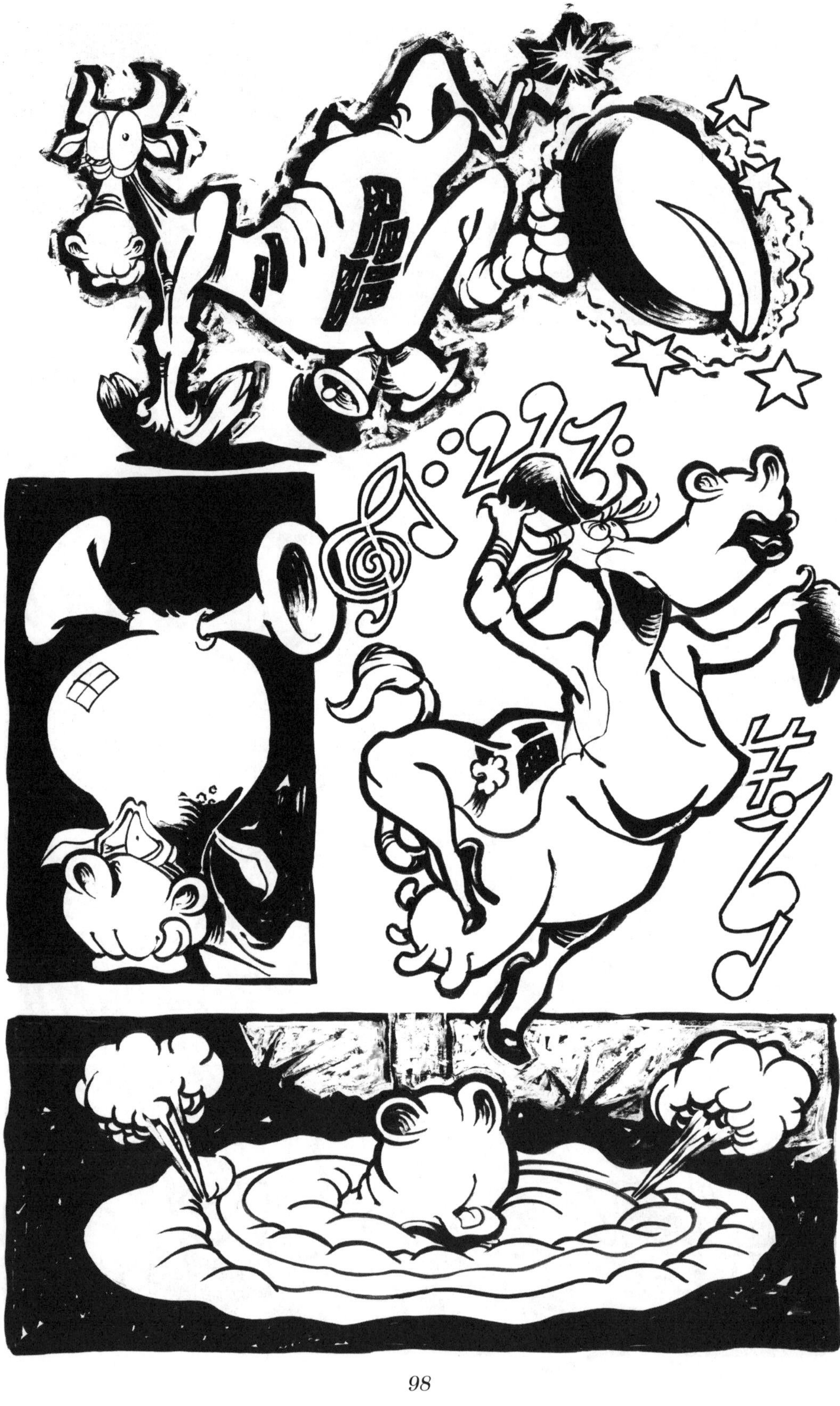

BY A SEASON OF JUDICIOUS NURSING, PHOEBE *the* COW WAS "BROUGHT ROUND ALL RIGHT"— AND WAS NOW AS TRACTABLE AND INOFFENSIVE AS A LITTLE CHILD.

SO MUCH SO, THAT ONE DAY MY AUNT PATIENCE DARED TO CONFIDENTLY GO UP TO HER TO SOOTHE HER WITH A PAN OF TURNIPS.

GAD! HOW THINLY SHE SPREAD THAT OLD LADY ON AN ADJACENT STONE WALL.

YOU COULD NOT HAVE DONE IT SO EASILY WITH A TROWEL.

the monk and the hangman's daughter

by Richard Voss / translated by Gustav Adolf Danziger
adapted by Ambrose Bierce
comics adaptation by Antonella Caputo
illustrated by Carlo Vergara

On the first of May in the year of our Blessed Lord 1680, the Franciscan monks Aegidius, Romanus and myself, Ambrosius, were sent by our Superior to the Monastery of Berchtesgaden, near Salzburg.

The Monastery was in a wild and mountainous country. Wherever we went we were greeted by the people in the name of our patron saint.

I, Brother Ambrosius, confess with shame that it seemed to me that the women sought more eagerly to kiss my hands –

– which surely was not right, since I was younger and less experienced than my companions.

When we stood at the opening of the pass into the mountains we were overcome with dejection; it looked like the mouth of Hell. Strengthening our hearts with prayers against evil spirits, we pressed forward.

At length we reached the bank of a stream. As we were about to cross the river, which was spanned by a rough bridge, I cast my eyes to the other shore where there was a meadow covered with flowers and in the center a gallows upon which hung the body of a man!

As we gazed in horror upon the dreadful spectacle, a young girl appeared. She glided towards the corpse waving her arms to scare away the birds of prey that had gathered about it.

COME BROTHERS, LET US HASTEN AND PRAY FOR THE SOUL OF THE DEAD.

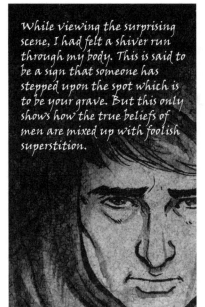

While viewing the surprising scene, I had felt a shiver run through my body. This is said to be a sign that someone has stepped upon the spot which is to be your grave. But this only shows how the true beliefs of men are mixed up with foolish superstition.

We soon said prayers for the sinner who hung above. Suddenly, in the midst of our devotions, I heard her sweet tones.

THE VULTURE!!

My brothers were indignant at the interruption.

GO TO HER AMBROSIUS, AND COMMAND HER TO BE SILENT THAT WE MAY PRAY IN PEACE FOR THE DEPARTED SOUL OF THIS SINFUL MAN!

WHO ARE YOU? AND WHAT ARE YOU DOING IN THIS DREADFUL PLACE?

EEEEEEEHHHHH!!!

She uttered a wild high scream and ran across the meadow so that I thought her mad.

I AM SCARING AWAY THE VULTURES. WHEN ANYONE IS HANGED HERE, I COME AND FRIGHTEN AWAY THE BIRDS.

The big bird flew away and the maiden came quietly back to me.

102

WHAT IS YOUR NAME, AND WHO ARE YOUR PARENTS?

BUT YOUR FATHER, WHERE IS HE?

BENEDICTA; MY MOTHER IS DEAD.

She pointed towards the pines. I saw among the trees a wretched hut, a habitation more fit for animals than human beings. Then I knew whose child she was.

SHE IS THE HANGMAN'S DAUGHTER.

Having prayed for the soul of the dead man, we left the accursed spot, but as we withdrew I looked back at the child of the hangman.

My companions reproved me for the interest that I manifested in her, but it made me sad to think this child was despised through no fault of her own.

Why should she be made to suffer blame because of her father's dreadful calling? I was named a dreamer who wished to overthrow the customs of the world.

103

Everyone, my brothers said, was bound to execrate the class to which the hangman and his family belonged, for all who associated with such persons would surely be contaminated.

At last we arrived at our destination. Upon the surface of the pine-covered rock was a cluster of huts and houses, the monastery in the midst. May the good God bless our entrance into this holy place.

I have now been in this wilderness for a few weeks. This house of our beloved Saint is a house of peace. And what happiness there will be for me when I am ordained as a priest of the Most High God! I think and dream of it and try to prepare my soul for that sacred gift.

Our superior, Father Andreas, is a mild and pious gentleman. Our brothers live in peace and harmony. All this region, and all it contains, belong to the monastery.

The most remarkable thing in this country is the salt-mining. The works give employment to the peasants, all under the command of the Saltmaster.

He has an only son; his name is Rochus, a handsome but wild and wicked youth.

I have again seen the hangman's daughter. As the bells were chiming for mass I saw her in front of the church. When she approached, the church people stepped aside, whispering and looking at her as if she were a leper. Compassion compelled me to approach her.

GOD GREET YOU, BENEDICTA.

I THANK YOU, MY LORD.

I AM NOT A **LORD** BUT A POOR SERVANT OF GOD, WHO IS A KIND FATHER TO ALL HIS CHILDREN, HOWEVER LOWLY THEIR ESTATE.

Out of the compassion in my heart, I led her into the church before all the people.

While Father Andreas was reciting the mass, my eyes wandered to the dark corner set aside for Benedicta and her father.

I feel for her a peculiar tenderness, which I cannot help accepting as a sign that I am charged to save her soul.

Our superior has sent for me to rebuke me. He told me I had caused great ill-feeling amongst the people.

WHY DID YOU PITY HER?

BECAUSE ALL THE PEOPLE SHUN HER!

IT IS NOT HER FAULT THAT HER FATHER IS A HANGMAN, NOR HIS EITHER, SINCE ALAS, HANGMEN MUST BE!

Ah, beloved Franciscus, how the superior scolded thy poor servant for these bold words.

He gave me a long lecture and put me under hard penance.

I took my punishment meekly, confined in my cell, fasting and chastising myself; but it is happiness to suffer for the sake of one so unjustly treated.

The monastery has celebrated a great festival. For many days before the event the monks were busy preparing the holy procession.

After us came a great crowd of people. The proudest of these were the salt miners, the Saltmaster at their head on a beautiful horse.

Behind him rode Rochus. He cast flaming glances upon the women. I fear he is not a good Christian.

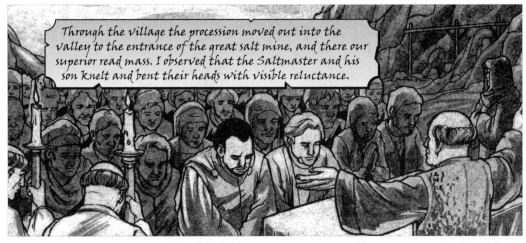

Through the village the procession moved out into the valley to the entrance of the great salt mine, and there our superior read mass. I observed that the Saltmaster and his son knelt and bent their heads with visible reluctance.

After the service came the feast. Tables had been provided for the Superior and the Fathers, and for the Saltmaster and the best of his people. I helped at table. I noticed how amorously the Saltmaster's son looked at the ladies, even those already married.

After eating, the young men played at various games. Foremost among all was the Saltmaster's son. Among these mountaineers he was a king.

ARE YOU THE MONK WHO GAVE OFFENSE TO THE PEOPLE THE OTHER DAY?

WHAT ARE YOU SPEAKING OF?

IF YOU EVER AGAIN SHOW ANY FRIENDSHIP TOWARDS THAT GIRL I SHALL TEACH YOU A LESSON WHICH YOU WILL NOT SOON FORGET!

I was alarmed to learn that this boy had cast his eyes upon the hangman's daughter.

I promised my blessed Saint that I would watch over and protect her.

The boys threw brushwood into the fire and began to swing the village maidens round. Rochus was dancing with a beautiful girl. She had a sensuous smile on her lips.

SEE! I AM THE MISTRESS OF YOUR HEART!

But suddenly he pushed her from him as if in disgust.

I AM GOING TO FETCH MY *OWN* PARTNER. WHO WILL GO WITH ME?

The tall girl stood looking at him with the face of a demon.

MONK, IF YOU CARE FOR THE HANGMAN'S DAUGHTER, THEN HASTEN AND SAVE HER.

I KNOW A PATH LEADING TO THE HANGMAN'S HUT BY A SHORTER ROUTE THAN THEY TAKE.

THEN SHOW ME, AND BE QUICK!

The girl, whose name was Amula, glided away. We were soon in the woods. Above us we could see the torches of the boys. I heard their wild shouts and trembled for the child.

THE HANGMAN IS ILL, AND UNABLE TO PROTECT HIS DAUGHTER.

THERE SHE LIVES. GO WARN HER.

With that she left and vanished in the darkness. Looking at the window I saw the hangman sitting in a chair. I could hear him cough and groan.

DO NOT FEAR, IT IS I — BROTHER AMBROSIUS.

ROCHUS IS WITH THEM. I HAVE COME TO ASSIST YOU TO ESCAPE. HASTEN, BENEDICTA, BE QUICK!

BENEDICTA, WILD AND DRUNKEN BOYS ARE ON THEIR WAY HITHER FROM THE DANCE...

Benedicta embraced her father, then she ran away into the woods. I entered the cabin to protect her father from the wild youths who, I thought, would visit their disappointment upon him.

Then I returned along the path by which I had come. As I neared the meadow, I could hear a madder uproar...

But they did not come. I waited and listened until the sounds died away in the distance. The sick man and I spoke of the miracle which had changed their hearts.

Holy Savior! There, in the midst of the dancing youths, were Rochus and Benedicta!

THE ACCURSED WENCH HAS RUN INTO ROCHUS' ARMS!

SHREEEEEEIIIIKKK..!!!

Amula could not control her rage, and rushed forward with a savage cry.

112

The drunken boys jeered at her and drove her away with curses and laughter.

When I saw the hatred in her eyes a cold shudder ran through my body.

I thought now to have gone home, but I was horrified to think of Rochus and Benedicta alone together in the forest.

Imagine my surprise when Benedicta lifted her head and looked kindly at Rochus...

I THANK YOU, SIR, FOR HAVING CHOSEN ME FOR YOUR PARTNER IN THE DANCE!

Before anyone could know, she disappeared in the black space of the forest.

Rochus raved like a madman. Observing my presence, he turned his wrath upon me.

I'LL MAKE YOU SMART FOR THIS, YOU MISERABLE COWL-WEARER!

But I do not fear him. Benedicta is not guilty and I can respect her as before. Ah, if I could be ever at her side to watch over her!

Again I am to be punished. Amula has been saying that Benedicta acted in the most shameless manner with the boys at the dance.

When the people spoke to me of this I enlightened them regarding the facts.

But this testimony in contradiction has offended the Superior.

IS IT NOT A FACT THAT SHE WENT OF HER OWN WILL TO JOIN THE DRUNKEN BOYS?

SHE WENT OUT OF LOVE FOR HER FATHER, WHO IS ILL AND HELPLESS, SO THE YOUTHS WOULD NOT MALTREAT HIM!

I was accused of defending the hangman's daughter against the word of an honest Christian girl, and his reverence put me under severe penance.

I willingly undergo it. I am glad to suffer for the sweet child.

Today is Sunday, and I have been released from my cell to celebrate mass. Benedicta was not in church, but Amula was among the maidens.

WHAT IS HAPPENING?

Following the mass, I heard a commotion in the street.

THEY ARE TAKING A WOMAN TO THE PILLORY.

WHAT HAS SHE DONE?

YOU ASK A FOOLISH QUESTION!

WHOM ARE PILLORIES AND WHIPPING-POSTS FOR, BUT FALLEN WOMEN?

The howling mob passed further into the square. Surrounded by this mob of screaming women, there was she, the sweet Benedicta!

THANK HEAVEN WE ARE VIRTUOUS!

SEE WHAT IT IS TO BE A SINNER!

Harlot

By the end of the rope around her waist Benedicta's father led her. They had compelled the poor man to lead his own child to the pillory!

Back in my cell, I cried aloud to God against the injustice that I had witnessed in my mind… the father binding his child to the post…

…the brutal populace cruelly dancing around her in savage delight…

…and the false and vicious Amula spitting in the pure one's face…

I sat and waited. The minutes seemed hours, the hours eternities. I was stunned and dazed.

Then it came like a revelation out of Heaven that my feeling for Benedicta is both more and less than what I thought of it…

It is an earthly love – that of a man for a woman. Yet does this human desire come not also of God?

Surely spiritual and earthly love are both but expressions of His will!

116

For some time I have been very ill, but by the kind attention of the brothers I am sufficiently recovered.

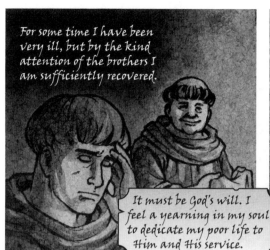

It must be God's will. I feel a yearning in my soul to dedicate my poor life to Him and His service.

I think unceasingly of the poor child of the hangman. What has become of her? I am not permitted to leave the monastery, and I don't dare ask her fate.

I am better and I have been called to the presence of Superior Andreas.

I HAVE ORDAINED THAT YOU LEAVE US FOR A SEASON TO DWELL APART IN THE SOLITUDE OF THE MOUNTAINS, THERE TO RESTORE YOUR STRENGTH AND AFFORD YOU AN INSIGHT INTO YOUR HEART...

PRAY THAT YOU MAY WALK UPRIGHT IN THE SERVICE OF THE LORD AS A TRUE APOSTLE, WITH IMMUNITY FROM BASE PASSIONS AND EARTHLY DESIRES.

I submitted to the will of His Reverence. In the mountains it will be my duty to dig the roots of gentiana and send them to the monastery.

From these roots the fathers distill a liquor that has become famous throughout the land.

A boy is to guide me to my solitary station. He will come once a week to renew my supply of food and take away the roots that I shall have dug.

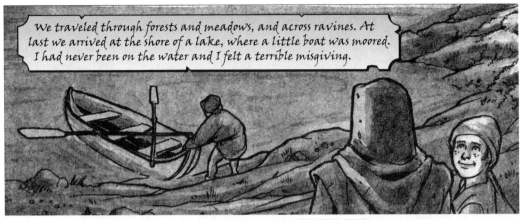

We traveled through forests and meadows, and across ravines. At last we arrived at the shore of a lake, where a little boat was moored. I had never been on the water and I felt a terrible misgiving.

As our boat crept on I observed the lake. The cliff rose to a great height, but to the left lay a pleasant land, where stood a large building. This was Saint Bartholomae, the summer residence of his Reverence, Superior Andreas.

We went ashore and climbed for hours until we reached a stream. Among the bare rocks I found a few flowers, the plants whose roots I am to dig.

We continued our journey and at last reached a lonely spot. In the center was a miserable hut of stones, and this was to be my habitation.

We entered, and my heart sank to think of dwelling in such a place.

The boy took up a pan and ran away with it. And throwing myself in front of the hut, I became lost in contemplation of the wildness and terror of the place.

But the boy soon returned with the pan full of milk, a pat of butter and a cake of cheese.

DO BUTTER AND CHEESE GROW ON STONE UP HERE, AND HAVE YOU FOUND A SPRING OF MILK?

YOU MIGHT ACCOMPLISH SUCH A MIRACLE, BUT I PREFER TO ASK THIS FOOD OF THE YOUNG WOMAN WHO LIVES BY THE BLACK LAKE.

THEN WE ARE NOT ALONE IN THIS WILDERNESS. WHERE IS THAT LAKE WHERE THIS GENEROUS PERSON DWELLS?

THE BLACK LAKE IS BEYOND THAT RISE...

"...IT IS A BAD PLACE. THE LAKE REACHES CLEAR DOWN TO HELL AND YOU CAN HEAR, THROUGH THE FISSURES OF THE ROCKS, THE HISSING OF THE FLAMES AND THE GROANS OF THE SOULS."

MILK AND BUTTER AND CHEESE CAN BE OBTAINED AT THE GREEN LAKE LOWER DOWN. I WILL TELL THE WOMEN TO SEND UP WHAT YOU REQUIRE.

THEY WILL BE GLAD TO OBLIGE YOU, IF YOU WILL PREACH A SERMON ON SUNDAYS.

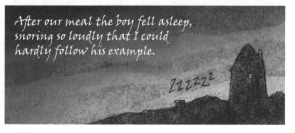

After our meal the boy fell asleep, snoring so loudly that I could hardly follow his example.

ZZZZZZ

When I woke up the young man had gone away and I was alone. Entering the cabin, I found a fire burning. Nor had he forgotten to prepare my supper for which I was truly grateful to him.

I emerged to a dawn more glorious than I had ever seen. I was kneeling in my morning devotions when I saw three female figures approaching.

They greeted me, and told me they were from the Green Lake. They kissed my hands after which they opened their baskets displaying the things they had brought me.

I enquired if they were not afraid to live in the wilderness. They said they had a gun in their cabin and knew anathemas against demons. They added that every Saturday the boys from the valley came up to hunt.

They went away as they had come, laughing and singing in the joy of youth. I believe that people in the mountains lead a happier life than those in the valley below.

I stowed away the provisions which they had brought me, and taking a spade and a bag, went in search of the gentiana roots.

I had gone a long distance from my cabin when suddenly I found myself on the brink of an abyss. At the bottom of the cabin a small circular lake was visible. On the shore of it stood a cabin. What a dreadful place for human habitation!

Then I heard a voice call a name! Soon I heard the voice again...

...and it caused my heart to beat so that I was near suffocation, for it was Benedicta's!

I spied her springing from rock to rock. When she saw me she stood motionless. Ah, how changed the poor child was!

IS IT YOU, BENEDICTA, WHO LIVES IN THE CABIN DOWN BY THE BLACK LAKE?

AND IS YOUR FATHER WITH YOU?

MY FATHER IS DEAD.

Stepping up to her, I took her hands in mine, and tried to crush back into my heart every human desire.

MY CHILD, YOUR FATHER IS GONE FROM YOU, BUT HE HAS GONE TO THE MERCY SEAT, AND GOD WILL BE GRACIOUS TO HIM.

But my words seemed only to awaken her sleeping sorrow, and she gave way to tears.

OH MY POOR FATHER! YES HE IS DEAD OF GRIEF.

MY MOTHER TOO, DIED OF GRIEF AND REMORSE FOR SOME GREAT SIN, I KNOW NOT WHAT, WHICH HE HAD FORGIVEN HER.

HIS HEART WAS TENDER, YET HE WAS COMPELLED TO KILL MEN. HIS FATHER AND HIS FATHER'S FATHER WERE HANGMEN, AND THE AWFUL INHERITANCE FELL TO HIM.

WHILE MY MOTHER WAS DYING MY FATHER IMPLORED THE REVEREND SUPERIOR TO SEND A PRIEST WITH THE SACRAMENT. HIS PRAYER WAS DENIED.

BEGONE, UNCLEAN SINNER!

I WAS BUT A YOUNG CHILD WHEN MY MOTHER DIED. NO PRIEST CAME, AND MY POOR FATHER CLOSED HER EYES HIMSELF.

ALL ALONE HE HAD TO DIG HER GRAVE. HE HAD NO OTHER PLACE THAN THE UNHOLY GROUND BENEATH THE GALLOWS. AND NOW MY FATHER HAS DIED UNSHRIVEN, AND HIS SOUL IS NOT WITH GOD, BUT BURNS IN FIRE!

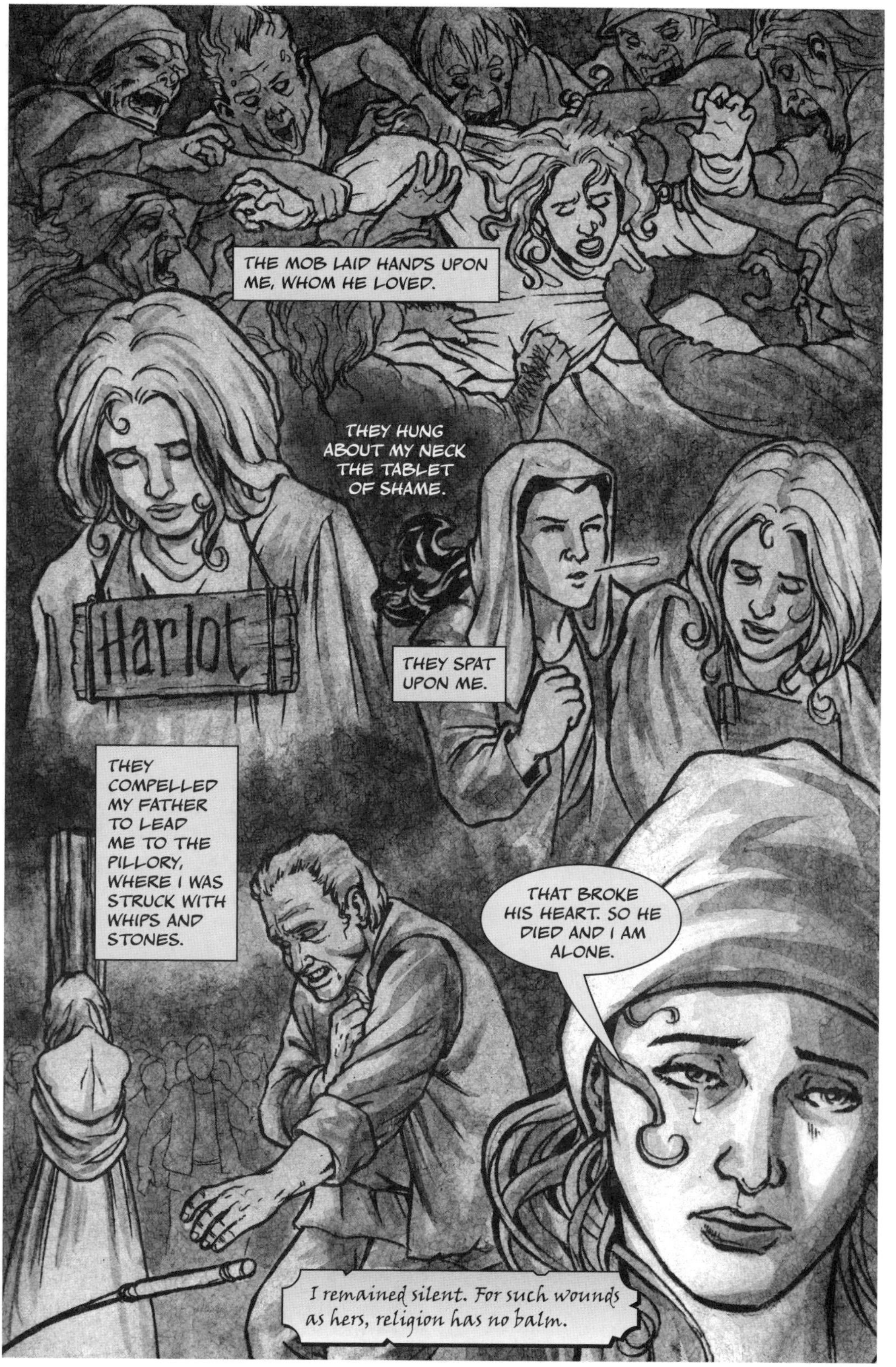
THE MOB LAID HANDS UPON ME, WHOM HE LOVED.
THEY HUNG ABOUT MY NECK THE TABLET OF SHAME.
Harlot
THEY SPAT UPON ME.
THEY COMPELLED MY FATHER TO LEAD ME TO THE PILLORY, WHERE I WAS STRUCK WITH WHIPS AND STONES.
THAT BROKE HIS HEART. SO HE DIED AND I AM ALONE.
I remained silent. For such wounds as hers, religion has no balm.

When Benedicta was composed, I inquired who the person was that I had heard her calling.

IT IS NO PERSON, IT IS ONLY MY GOAT. SHE HAS STRAYED AWAY, AND I WAS SEARCHING FOR HER AMONG THE ROCKS.

We soon discovered the animal in a crevice.

BAAAAAHHH!

HER MOTHER FELL FROM A CLIFF AND DIED. I TOOK CARE OF THIS LITTLE ONE.

NEXT SUNDAY I SHALL PREACH TO THE DAIRY WOMEN FROM THE GREEN LAKE, WILL YOU COME?

I SHOULD LIKE TO COME, BUT I CANNOT. MY PRESENCE WOULD FRIGHTEN AWAY THOSE WOMEN.

AND NOW GOODBYE, BROTHER.

Reflecting upon the cruel wrongs done to Benedicta, I became conscious of the nature of my love for her.

SAVE ME, O LORD! I AM ENGULFED IN A GREAT PASSION. SAVE ME, OR I PERISH FOREVER!

It was plain to me that unless my love for that child should be changed to a spiritual affection, I should _never_ receive holy orders.

All that night I fought against the evil spirit in my soul. At the dawning of the day I became more tranquil, and peace once more filled my heart.

The night before the Sunday on which I was to hold divine service great fires were kindled on the cliff, a signal for the young men in the valley to come up to the mountain dairies.

The monastery boy came in with the rest, and he gave me much news.

One piece of news that gives me alarm is that the Saltmaster's son is hunting in the mountains not far from the Black Lake.

Would that an angel might guard the path to the lake... and to Benedicta!

Early next morning the boys and girls arrived from all directions. Not being an ordained priest, it was not permitted for me to read mass, but I prayed with them and spoke of God's great mercy.

The next day the Superior sent for me. With a strange foreboding I followed his messenger.

Occupied with gloomy reflections, I hardly observed that we had left the shore before the sound of merry voices apprised me of our arrival at St. Bartholomae.

I was instructed to wait until after supper, when I was conducted to the Superior's apartment.

HOW FARES YOUR SOUL, MY SON AMBROSIUS? HAS THE LORD SHOWN YOU GRACE?

MOST REVEREND FATHER, GOD, IN MY SOLITUDE, HAS GIVEN ME KNOWLEDGE.

I HAVE GOOD TIDINGS FOR YOU. I HAVE WRITTEN ON YOUR BEHALF TO THE BISHOP OF SALZBURG. HE WILL CONSECRATE YOU AND GIVE YOU HOLY ORDERS, AND YOU WILL REMAIN IN HIS CITY.

PREPARE YOURSELF, FOR IN THREE DAYS YOU ARE TO LEAVE US.

I am to go away forever, and I must renounce my protection of Benedicta. God help her – and me!

I am once more in my mountain home, but tomorrow I leave. Now that my ambition is almost within my grasp, I find I am sad beyond measure. If I could become a priest, I could be Benedicta's confessor and absolve her from sin.

If I could place her under thy protection, O Blessed Virgin, that would be happiness indeed.

I have been to Benedicta's cabin.

BENEDICTA, I AM GOING AWAY FROM HERE. POOR CHILD, WHAT WILL BECOME OF YOU? THERE IS NO SAFETY FOR YOU BUT IN CLINGING TO THE CROSS OF OUR SAVIOUR.

YOU WRONG HIM, SIR, INDEED YOU DO.

BUT I KNOW THAT YOUR LOVE FOR THE WICKED ROCHUS IS STRONG.

THEN WHY DID HE NOT STAND FORTH AND DEFEND YOU WHEN YOU WERE FALSELY ACCUSED?

HE AND HIS FATHER WERE IN SALZBURG. HE KNEW NOTHING 'TIL LATER.

BUT HE DOES NOT SEEK YOU WITH HONORABLE PURPOSE. WILL HE TAKE FOR A WIFE ONE WHOSE GOOD NAME HAS BEEN BLACKENED IN THE SIGHT OF HIS FAMILY AND NEIGHBORS?

She remained silent. I saw that she was too weak to resist the temptation to love Rochus, and my soul melted with pity for her and sorrow for myself.

TAKE AN OATH THAT YOU WOULD THROW YOURSELF INTO THE WATERS OF THE BLACK LAKE RATHER THAN INTO THE ARMS OF ROCHUS!

Benedicta fixed her eyes upon mine with a look of sadness and reproach. Turning away, I left her.

I returned to my cabin and packed. The walls seemed too narrow to hold me; the air too heavy to sustain life.

Going outside, I walked in the darkness. An invisible hand directed my steps; and although it led me to my death, I know it to have been the hand of the Lord.

Walking on, I found myself at the foot of the precipice.

Here was a narrow path leading upward; and I began ascending it. After some distance I saw a cabin. This was the hunting lodge of the Saltmaster's son. I would wait for him here.

I crouched in the shadows and waited, thinking what to say to him to change his heart and turn him from his evil purpose.

Finally he came.

WHAT DO YOU WANT?

I replied mildly, explaining why I barred his way, and begging him to go back.

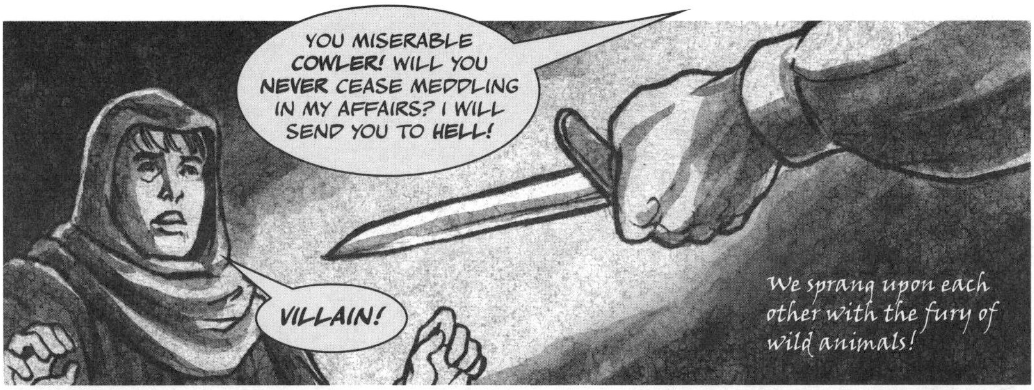
YOU MISERABLE COWLER! WILL YOU NEVER CEASE MEDDLING IN MY AFFAIRS? I WILL SEND YOU TO HELL!
VILLAIN!
We sprang upon each other with the fury of wild animals!

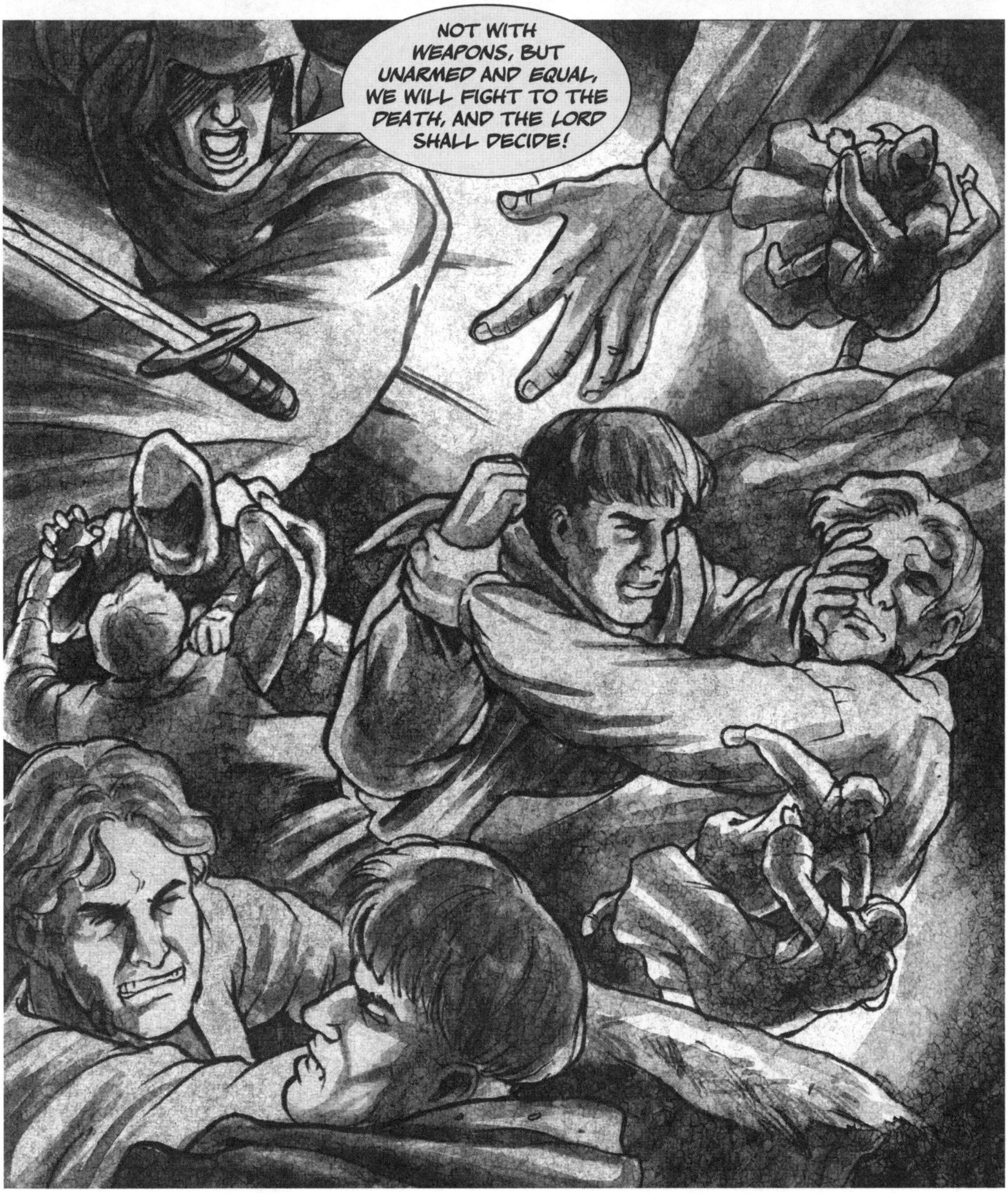
NOT WITH WEAPONS, BUT UNARMED AND EQUAL, WE WILL FIGHT TO THE DEATH, AND THE LORD SHALL DECIDE!

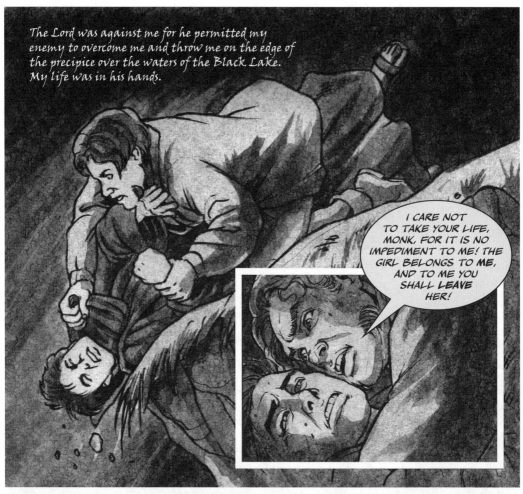

The Lord was against me for he permitted my enemy to overcome me and throw me on the edge of the precipice over the waters of the Black Lake. My life was in his hands.

I CARE NOT TO TAKE YOUR LIFE, MONK, FOR IT IS NO IMPEDIMENT TO ME! THE GIRL BELONGS TO ME, AND TO ME YOU SHALL **LEAVE** HER!

With that, he rose and proceeded down the path towards the lake.

Finally I was able to rise; I could still feel the fierce youth's knee upon my breast. I walked with difficulty back along the path.

At one point there was a break in the wall of the cliff, a great crevice that clove the mountain.

Here I remained for three days and two nights.

BROTHER AMBROSIUS! WHERE ARE YOU?

I heard the boy from the monastery calling my name, but I made no answer.

Not once did I quench my thirst at the brook or appease my hunger with blackberries.

I mortified my sinful flesh until at last I felt myself freed from the bondage of earthly love.

I devote my life to no woman but thee, O Blessed Virgin!

I was no longer myself. Ambrosius, the poor errant monk, was dead.

I was an instrument in the hand of God to execute His holy will.

The Lord commanded me to rise; to leave the scene of my purgatory and to regain the path that led up the face of the cliff.

Suddenly I felt impelled to stop and look down, and there at my feet lay the knife of Rochus. Now I understood why the Lord had permitted the wicked youth to conquer me. I had been reserved for a more glorious purpose.

I continued towards the Black Lake.

Benedicta's door was ajar. I stood outside, gazing upon the beautiful picture presented to my eyes.

Opposite the fire sat Benedicta, combing her long golden hair while she sang. But though her voice was that of an angel, it angered me.

She sprang up and manifested joy at seeing me.

But she had no sooner glanced into my face than she uttered a scream of terror as if I had been a fiend from Hell!

EEEEEEKKK!!!

WHY DO YOU SING, BENEDICTA, AND ARRANGE YOUR HAIR AS IF YOU EXPECTED YOUR LOVER?

WHY DO YOU ADORN YOURSELF SO LATE IN THE NIGHT?

HAVE THE THREE DAYS OF MY ABSENCE BEEN LONG ENOUGH FOR YOU TO FALL?

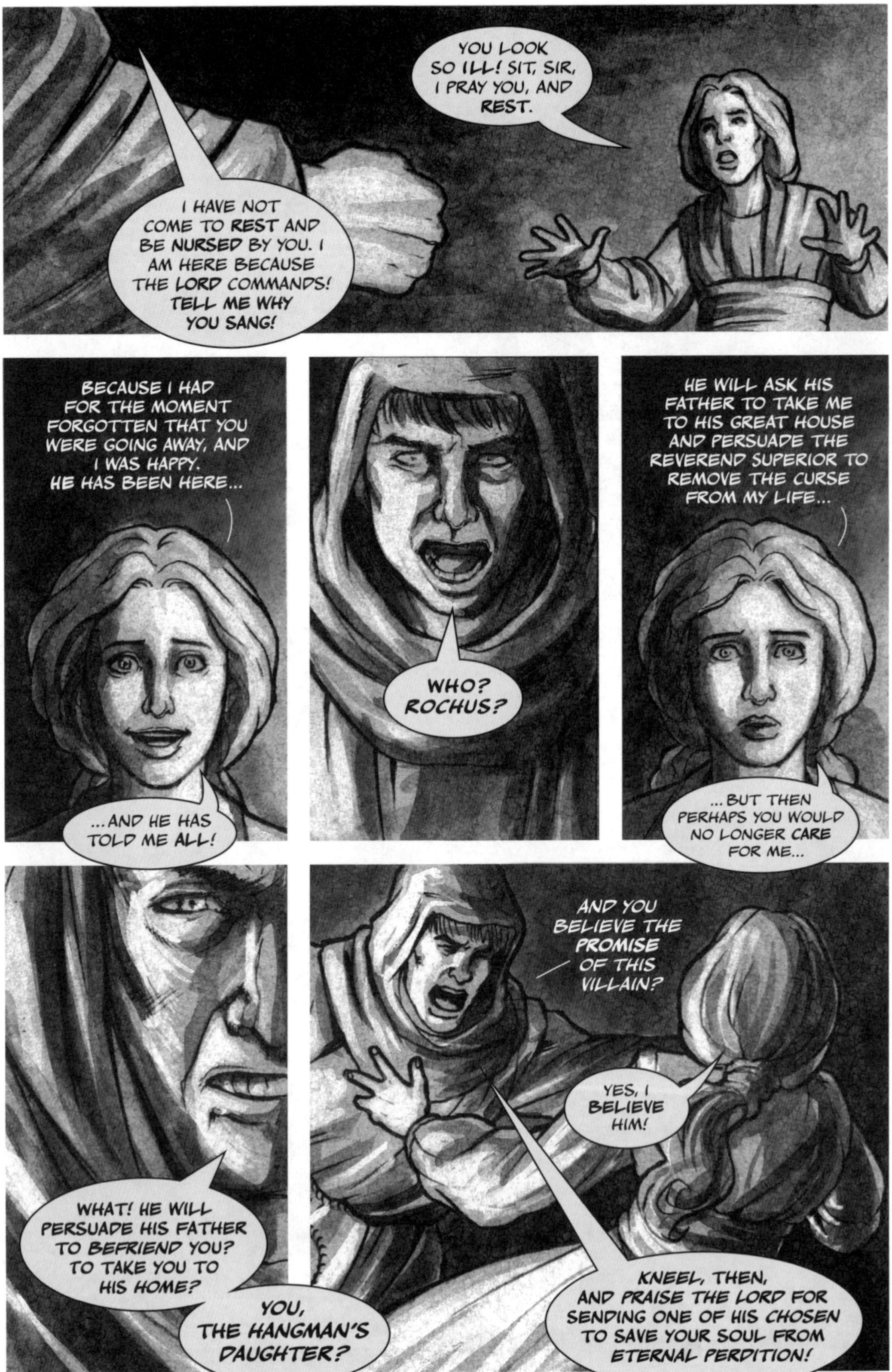
YOU LOOK SO ILL! SIT, SIR, I PRAY YOU, AND REST.
I HAVE NOT COME TO REST AND BE NURSED BY YOU. I AM HERE BECAUSE THE LORD COMMANDS! TELL ME WHY YOU SANG!
BECAUSE I HAD FOR THE MOMENT FORGOTTEN THAT YOU WERE GOING AWAY, AND I WAS HAPPY. HE HAS BEEN HERE...
...AND HE HAS TOLD ME ALL!
WHO? ROCHUS?
HE WILL ASK HIS FATHER TO TAKE ME TO HIS GREAT HOUSE AND PERSUADE THE REVEREND SUPERIOR TO REMOVE THE CURSE FROM MY LIFE...
...BUT THEN PERHAPS YOU WOULD NO LONGER CARE FOR ME...
WHAT! HE WILL PERSUADE HIS FATHER TO BEFRIEND YOU? TO TAKE YOU TO HIS HOME?
YOU, THE HANGMAN'S DAUGHTER?
AND YOU BELIEVE THE PROMISE OF THIS VILLAIN?
YES, I BELIEVE HIM!
KNEEL, THEN, AND PRAISE THE LORD FOR SENDING ONE OF HIS CHOSEN TO SAVE YOUR SOUL FROM ETERNAL PERDITION!

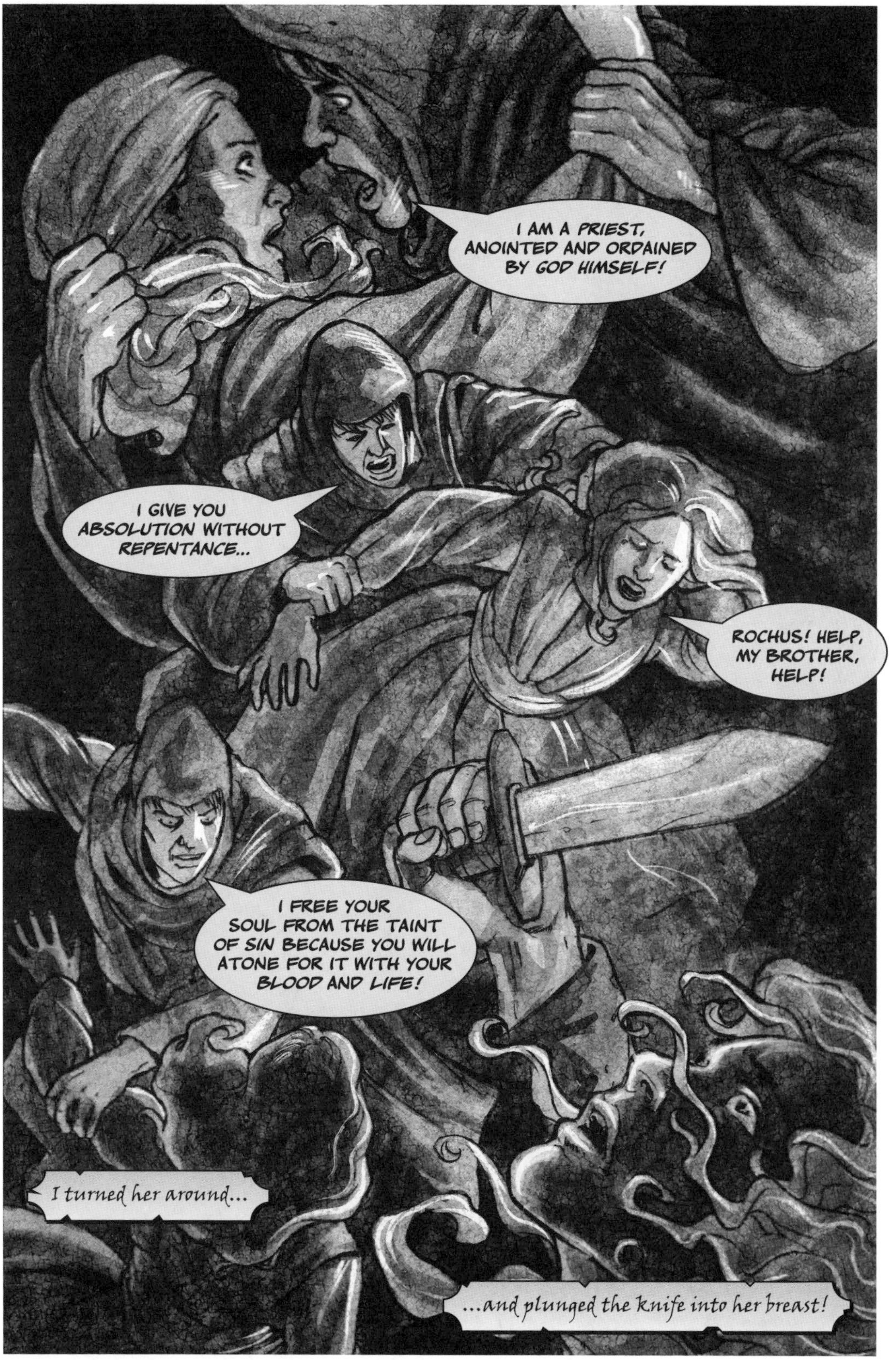
I AM A PRIEST, ANOINTED AND ORDAINED BY GOD HIMSELF!
I GIVE YOU ABSOLUTION WITHOUT REPENTANCE...
ROCHUS! HELP, MY BROTHER, HELP!
I FREE YOUR SOUL FROM THE TAINT OF SIN BECAUSE YOU WILL ATONE FOR IT WITH YOUR BLOOD AND LIFE!
I turned her around...
...and plunged the knife into her breast!

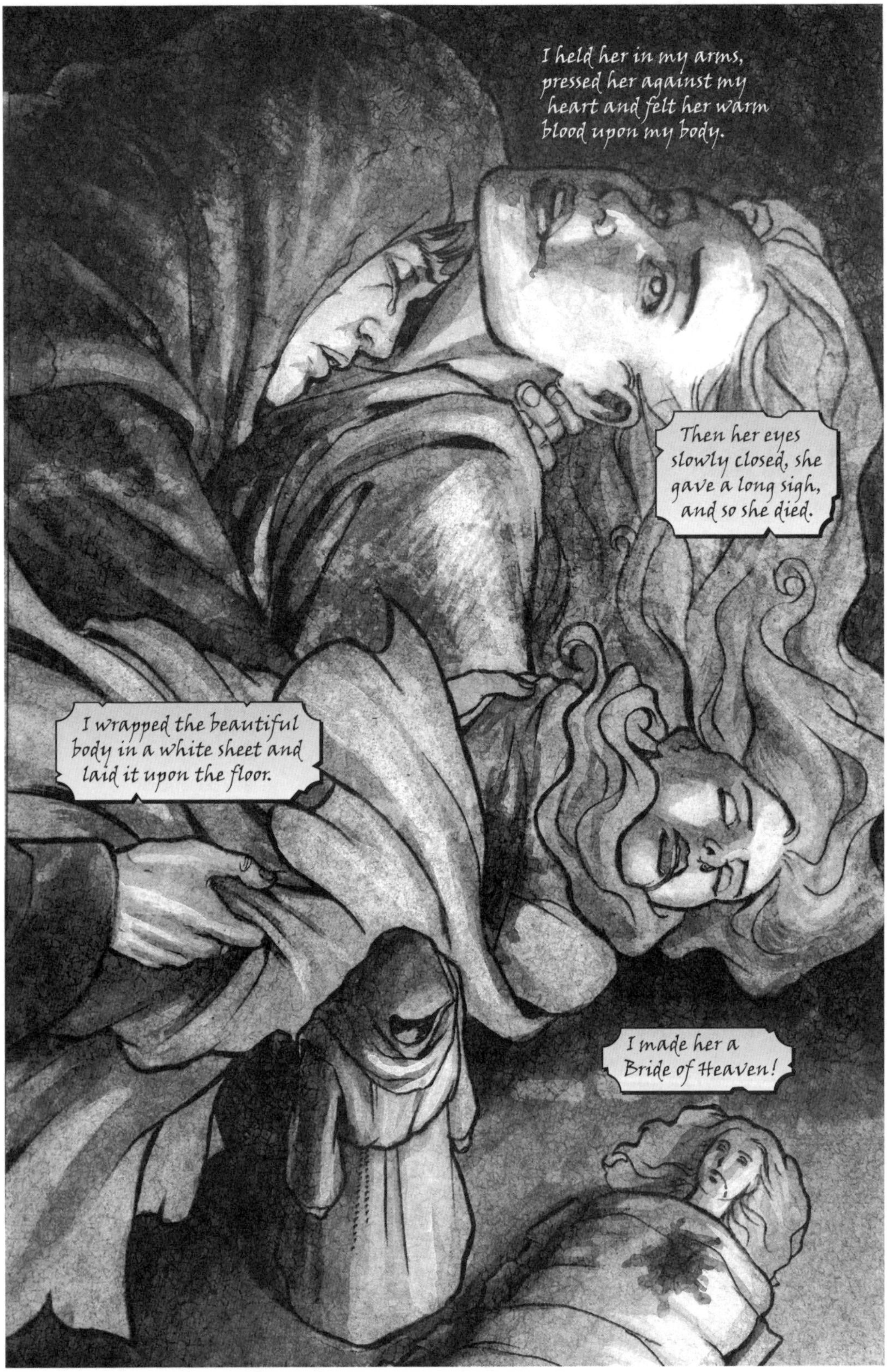
I held her in my arms, pressed her against my heart and felt her warm blood upon my body.
Then her eyes slowly closed, she gave a long sigh, and so she died.
I wrapped the beautiful body in a white sheet and laid it upon the floor.
I made her a Bride of Heaven!

I descended the mountain, and at the dawning of the day I arrived at the monastery.

The porter evidently thought me a fiend, for he raised a howl that aroused the whole population.

HELP! BROTHERS...!

I went straight to the room of the Superior.

THE LORD HAS CHOSEN ME!

...I AM NOW AN ORDAINED PRIEST!!

At this they seized me, and put me in the tower.

They condemned me to death as if I were a murderer. Oh, the fools!

One person came to me in my dungeon — who adored me as God's chosen instrument.

Amula alone has discovered that I have done a great and glorious deed.

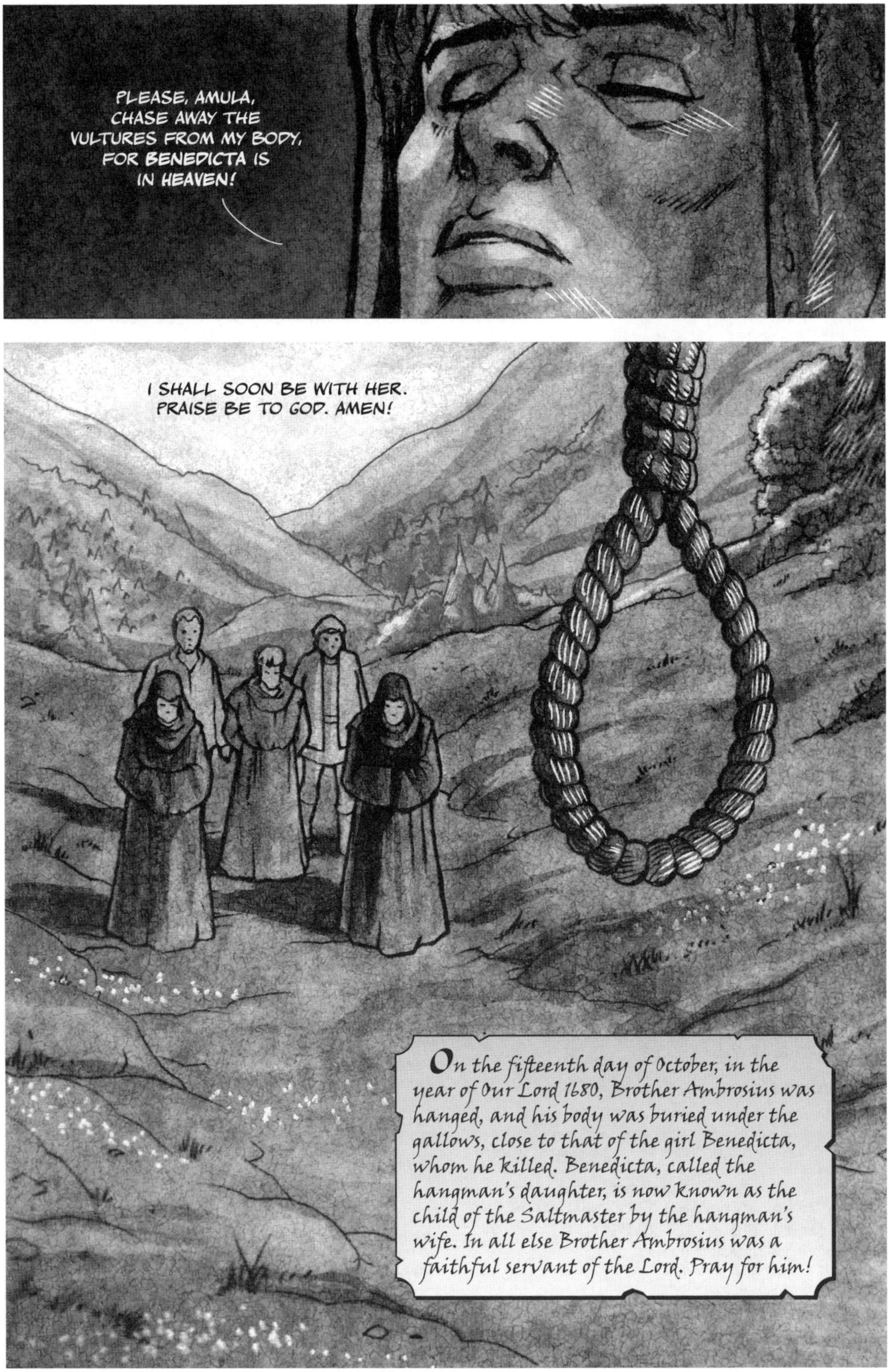
PLEASE, AMULA, CHASE AWAY THE VULTURES FROM MY BODY, FOR BENEDICTA IS IN HEAVEN!
I SHALL SOON BE WITH HER. PRAISE BE TO GOD. AMEN!
On the fifteenth day of October, in the year of Our Lord 1680, Brother Ambrosius was hanged, and his body was buried under the gallows, close to that of the girl Benedicta, whom he killed. Benedicta, called the hangman's daughter, is now known as the child of the Saltmaster by the hangman's wife. In all else Brother Ambrosius was a faithful servant of the Lord. Pray for him!

AMBROSE BIERCE

Born in rural Ohio in 1842, Bierce became a printer's apprentice for a small Indiana newspaper until 1860, when he enlisted in the Union army. He witnessed some of the major battles of the Civil War, and in 1864, at Kenesaw Mountain, was shot in the head and left for dead. Bierce recovered, though with lingering effects to his health. He remained in the army during the Reconstruction and a later mapping expedition in the West. When the mapping party reached San Francisco, Bierce was denied an expected promotion and resigned from the military in disgust. He then decided to pursue a career in journalism. He accepted a position as a columnist with the *San Francisco News Letter and Commercial Advertiser* and from there went on to edit *The Wasp*, a journal of humor, politics and literature. He later became associated with publisher William Randolph Hearst, and worked for the *San Francisco Examiner*, the *New York Journal* and *Cosmopolitan*. The selections from *The Devil's Dictionary* in this volume, and most of the short pieces and poems collected under the title *Bierce's Fables*, originally appeared in Bierce's newspaper and magazine columns. Examples of each are featured in this volume. In his time, Bierce was a celebrity as a satirical columnist, but disappointment over a lack of acceptance of his fiction and a troubled personal life, including a divorce and the death of his two sons, caused him to become increasingly bitter and withdrawn in his later years. In 1913, at the age of 71, he crossed the border into Mexico, "with a pretty definite purpose, which, however, is not at present disclosable." He was never heard from again.

More stories by Ambrose Bierce are adapted in
Horror Classics: Graphic Classics Volume Ten
Graphic Classics: Special Edition

STEVEN CERIO *(cover, page 38)*

Steven Cerio's work spans all mediums from magazine and book illustrations to toy design, animation and film. His artwork has been shown in galleries throughout the U.S. and Europe, and his illustration clients include Nickelodeon, A&M Records, Disney, 20th Century Fox, Warner Bros, *Entertainment Weekly*, *Newsweek* and *Time*. He has created posters and other graphics for numerous musical acts and has long been involved artistically with legendary San Francisco psychedelic group The Residents. Steven's first full-length comic book, *PIE*, came out in 1996, and the award-winning *Steven Cerio's ABC Book, A Drug Primer* was published in 1998. He is currently concentrating on his children's books and other varied projects that include recording his second album for Noiseville Records with his group Atlantic Drone, teaching at Syracuse University's College of Art, and creating his first comic in eight years.

See more at www.happyhomelandstore.com and in
Graphic Classics: Edgar Allan Poe

J.B. BONIVERT *(pages 1, 52, 80)*

Jeff Bonivert is a Bay Area native who has contributed to independent comics as both artist and writer, in such books as *The Funboys*, *Turtle Soup* and *Mister Monster*. Jeff's biography of artist Murphy Anderson appears in *Spark Generators*, and *Muscle and Faith*, his Casey Jones/Teenage Mutant Ninja Turtles epic, can be seen online at www.flyingcolorscomics.com.

Jeff's work has appeared in
Graphic Classics: Edgar Allan Poe
Graphic Classics: Arthur Conan Doyle
Graphic Classics: H.P. Lovecraft
Graphic Classics: Jack London
Graphic Classics: Bram Stoker
Adventure Classics: Graphic Classics Volume Twelve

FLORENCE CESTAC *(page 2)*

Born in 1949, Florence Cestac studied art in Rouen and Paris. She co-founded Bonbel, an artist collective in Rouen, and in 1972 she co-founded the bookstore Futuropolis and later a publishing company with the same name. Her comic character "Harry Mickson" became the company's emblem and mascot. Cestac's work has appeared in magazines including *Ah Nana!*, *Métal Hurlant*, *Charlie Mensuel*, *Pilote* and *Chic*. Her books include *Cauchemar Matinal*, *Comment Faire de la Bédé*, *La Guerre des Boutons*, *Le Démon de Midi*, *Je Veux Pas Divorcer* and *Survivre & Noël*. Her comics autobiography *La Vie D'Artiste* was published in 2002 by Dargaud.

More illustration by Florence Cestac appears in
Graphic Classics: Mark Twain

CARLO VERGARA *(pages 3, 100, back cover)*

Carlo Vergara (carverhouse.blogspot.com) is a graphic designer based in the Philippines, who has moonlighted as stage actor and university lecturer. His original graphic novel, *The Spectacular Adventures of Zsazsa Zaturnnah*, won a National Book Award from the Manila Critics Circle in 2003, and has since been adapted as a musical stage production and a major motion picture. He is currently developing a sequel to the Zaturnnah story.

Carlo has also illustrated adaptations in
Graphic Classics: Rafael Sabatini
Gothic Classics: Graphic Classics Volume Fourteen

ROD LOTT *(page 4)*

Oklahoma City resident Rod Lott is a freelance writer and graphic designer working in advertising and journalism. For twelve years, he has published and edited the more-or-less quarterly magazine *Hitch: The Journal of Pop Culture Absurdity* (www.hitchmagazine.com), and edits *Bookgasm*, a daily book review and news site at www.bookgasm.com. Rod's humorous essays have been published in several anthologies, including *May Contain Nuts* and *101 Damnations*.

You can learn more about his work at www.rodlott.com, and you can find more comics adaptations by Rod Lott in
Graphic Classics: Edgar Allan Poe
Graphic Classics: Arthur Conan Doyle
Graphic Classics: H.G. Wells
Graphic Classics: H.P. Lovecraft
Graphic Classics: Jack London
Graphic Classics: O. Henry
Graphic Classics: Rafael Sabatini
Horror Classics: Graphic Classics Volume Ten
Adventure Classics: Graphic Classics Volume Twelve
Gothic Classics: Graphic Classics Volume Fourteen
Fantasy Classics: Graphic Classics Volume Fifteen
Graphic Classics: Special Edition

RENO MANIQUIS *(page 4)*

Reno has been writing and illustrating short stories for comics in his native Philippines since age thirteen. During his college days, he created the newspaper strip *Maskarado* (Masked Man) and in the late '90s he revived the character as a self-published comic book. He has contributed to various publications in the Philippines, including the award-winning anthology *Siglo: Passion*, *Colors Magazine* in Europe, and independent publishers in the U.S. including 803 Studios' *Sequential Suicide: Slop* and Ultimate Comics' *Stormblazer*. He has also also published *Tabloid Komiks*, an anthology which showcases stories and art from Filipino creators. Reno works as an advertising industry art director, and is currently the regular artist on *Wall of Angels*, published by Twenty To Six Books. You can find his work online at ka-blog.blogspot.com and www.capsulezone.tk. "The Damned Thing" is his first work for *Graphic Classics*.

MORT CASTLE (page 16)

A writing teacher and author specializing in the horror genre, Mort Castle has written and edited fourteen books and around 500 short stories and articles. His novels and collections include *Cursed Be the Child*, *The Strangers*, *Moon on the Water* and *Nations of the Living, Nations of the Dead*, and he is the author of the essential reference work for aspiring horror writers, *Writing Horror*. Mort has won numerous writing awards, and he has had several dozen stories cited in "year's best" compilations in the horror, suspense, fantasy, and literary fields. He has been a writer and editor for several comics publishers, is a frequent keynote speaker at writing conferences and is currently the editor of *Doorways Magazine*.

Mort has contributed work to
Graphic Classics: Jack London
Graphic Classics: Robert Louis Stevenson
Graphic Classics: O. Henry
Graphic Classics: Rafael Sabatini

DAN E. BURR (page 16)

Together with author James Vance, Dan Burr is a winner of the comic industry's Eisner and Harvey awards for the graphic novel *Kings In Disguise*. Dan has also produced a number of historical comics for the DC/Paradox *Big Book* series, and he has worked extensively for Golden Books and other publishers doing illustrations for children's educational materials. "The Disappearance of Ambrose Bierce" is an homage by Dan and Mort Castle to the style of *Mad Magazine's* great Will Elder. Of late, Dan has been concentrating his time on portraiture and caricature work.

STAN SHAW (page 20)

Stan Shaw (drawstanley.com) illustrates for various clients all over the country including *The Village Voice, Esquire, Slate, Starbucks, The Seattle Mariners, Nintendo, Rhino Records, Microsoft, R.E.I., B.E.T., P.O.V., DC Comics,* ABCNEWS.com, *Wizards of The Coast, Amazing Stories, Vibe, The Flying Karamazov Brothers* and *Willamette Week*. In addition to practicing illustration, he teaches it, at Cornish School of the Arts, School of Visual Concepts and Pacific Lutheran University. He is now part of a group of artists advising on an illustration textbook.

Stan can be reached at drawstanley@harbornet.com. He has illustrated stories in
Graphic Classics: Edgar Allan Poe
Graphic Classics: O. Henry
Graphic Classics: Rafael Sabatini

MARK A. NELSON (page 31)

Mark Nelson was a professor of art at Northern Illinois University for twenty years. From 1998 to 2004 he was a senior artist at Raven Software, doing conceptual work, painting digital skins and creating textures for computer games. Mark is now the lead instructor of the Animation Department of Madison Area Technical College in Madison, Wisconsin. His comics credits include *Blood and Shadows* for DC, *Aliens* for Dark Horse Comics, and *Feud* for Marvel. He has worked for numerous publishers, and his art is represented in *Spectrum #4, 5, 6, 8, 10* and his art collections *From Pencils to Inks: The Art of Mark A. Nelson* (2004) and *Strange Thoughts and Random Images* (2008).

Mark's comics and illustrations appear in
Graphic Classics: H.P. Lovecraft
Graphic Classics: Jack London
Graphic Classics: O. Henry
Graphic Classics: Bram Stoker
Horror Classics: Graphic Classics Volume Ten
Fantasy Classics: Graphic Classics Volume Fifteen

MICHAEL SLACK (page 46)

Michael Slack is an illustrator and animator whose work has appeared in publications including *The New York Times, Nickelodeon Magazine* and *Time Magazine*. He has designed characters for Aardman Animation and Passion Pictures in the U.K., and his first book, *The Land of O*, received a 2002 Xeric Foundation grant. He is currently working on personal projects, including a card game, children's books and gallery exhibitions.

He can be contacted at www.slackart.com, and seen in
Graphic Classics: Robert Louis Stevenson
Graphic Classics: O. Henry

SHARY FLENNIKEN (page 53)

Shary Flenniken is a cartoonist, editor, author and screenwriter. She is best known for her irreverent comic strip *Trots & Bonnie*, about precocious preteens, which appeared in various underground comics and *National Lampoon*. Shary's graphic stories and comic strips have appeared in *Details, Premiere, Harvey,* and *Mad* magazines, as well as in *Graphic Classics: H.G. Wells, Graphic Classics: Ambrose Bierce, Graphic Classics: Mark Twain, Graphic Classics: Robert Louis Stevenson* and *Graphic Classics: O. Henry*. Her artwork can also be seen in *When a Man Loves A Walnut, More Misheard Lyrics* by the "very cool" Gavin Edwards, *Nice Guys Sleep Alone* by "big-time loser" Bruce Feirstein, and *Seattle Laughs*, a "truly wonderful" book edited by Shary. She is currently teaching comedy writing and cartooning while working on a book of fairy tales and a series of novels that she claims are "not even remotely autobiographical." You can contact Shary and find out how to purchase original artwork at www.sharyflenniken.com.

See more of Shary's comics and illustrations in
Graphic Classics: Mark Twain
Graphic Classics: Robert Louis Stevenson
Graphic Classics: O. Henry
Gothic Classics: Graphic Classics Volume Fourteen

ANTONELLA CAPUTO (pages 54, 100)

Antonella was born and raised in Rome, Italy, and now lives in Lancaster, England. She has been an architect, archaeologist, art restorer, photographer, calligrapher, interior designer, theater designer, actress and theater director. Her first published work was *Casa Montesi*, a fortnightly comic strip which appeared in the national magazine *Il Giornalino*. She has since written comedies for children and scripts for comics and magazines in the UK, Europe and the U.S.

Antonella works with Nick Miller as the writing half of Team Sputnik, and has collaborated with Nick and other artists in
Graphic Classics: Edgar Allan Poe
Graphic Classics: Arthur Conan Doyle
Graphic Classics: H.G. Wells
Graphic Classics: Jack London
Graphic Classics: Mark Twain
Graphic Classics: O. Henry
Graphic Classics: Rafael Sabatini
Horror Classics: Graphic Classics Volume Ten
Adventure Classics: Graphic Classics Volume Twelve
Gothic Classics: Graphic Classics Volume Fourteen
Fantasy Classics: Graphic Classics Volume Fifteen
Graphic Classics: Special Edition

NICK MILLER (page 54)

Nick grew up in the depths of rural England, and now lives in Lancaster with his partner, Antonella Caputo. The son of two artists, he learned to draw at an early age. After leaving art school he worked as a graphic designer before switching to cartooning and illustration full-time in the early '90s. Since then his work has appeared in many

ILLUSTRATION ©2003 ANTON EMDIN

comics and magazines in the U.K., U.S. and Europe, as well as in comic anthologies, websites and in advertising. His weekly comic strip, *The Really Heavy Greatcoat*, can be seen online at www.lancasterukonline.net. He works as part of Team Sputnik with Antonella Caputo, and also independently with other writers including John Freeman, Tony Husband, Mark Rogers and Tim Quinn.

Nick's stories have appeared in
Graphic Classics: Arthur Conan Doyle
Graphic Classics: H.G. Wells
Graphic Classics: Jack London
Graphic Classics: Mark Twain
Horror Classics: Graphic Classics Volume Ten
Adventure Classics: Graphic Classics Volume Twelve

MARK DANCEY *(page 56)*

Mark Dancey was born in Ann Arbor, Michigan in 1963. "For no good reason," Mr. Dancey co-founded the satirical and highly influential *Motorbooty Magazine* in the late 1980s and filled its pages with his comics and illustrations. In the 1990s and 2000s his work appeared "in many glossy consumer magazines and in the hep galleries of our most glamorous cities." Mark now lives in southwest Detroit, where he produces painstaking works in oil and prints posters under the aegis of his company, Iluminado. He is presently working on *Mythographic*, a volume of illustrated mythology.

You are cordially invited to visit Mark at his website www.iluminado.us, and view his work in
Graphic Classics: Mark Twain
Horror Classics: Graphic Classics Volume Ten
Graphic Classics: Special Edition

NEALE BLANDEN
(page 57)

Neale lives in Melbourne, Australia and has been self-publishing comics since 1988. He has appeared in comics anthologies around the globe, and his artwork has been exhibited in galleries in Australia, Canada and Europe. He currently is teaching cartooning, animation and storyboarding at the college level.

Neale's unique style can also be seen in
Graphic Classics: Robert Louis Stevenson

JACKIE SMITH *(page 58)*

Jackie Smith is from Sheffield, in northern England. She originally trained as an animator and has drawn comics since the late 1970s. She's been a T-shirt designer, graphic artist and Youth Arts Worker and a freelance cartoonist, writer and illustrator since 1980. Her best work has appeared in *Knockabout Comics*. Other long-term contracts have been with *Big Mags* and *Myatt McFarlane*. She also takes comics and illustration into schools and has used *Graphic Classics* in her work with excluded teenagers. Jackie enjoys drawing caricatures and portraits at fairs and occasionally sneaks off to the wild peaks to paint landscapes. Present projects include a graphic novel and a series of portraits of scary teenagers.

Jackie has also illustrated for
Graphic Classics: Rafael Sabatini
Horror Classics: Graphic Classics Volume Ten

DAN O'NEILL *(page 60)*

In 1963 Dan O'Neill dropped out of college and started his comic strip *Odd Bodkins* for the *San Francisco Chronicle*. For seven years O'Neill proceeded to entertain readers and offend editors before finally being fired. These strips are collected in two books, *Hear the Sound of My Feet Walking Drown the Sound of My Voice Talking* and *The Collective Unconscience of Odd Bodkins*. In 1970, at the height of the underground comix movement, O'Neill met four cartoonists who would form the core of his infamous comics collective, The Air Pirates: Ted Richards, Gary Hallgren, Bobby London and Shary Flenniken. They produced comics which consisted largely of satires of Disney cartoon characters. O'Neill's intent was to provoke a reaction from the Disney empire and in 1971 he succeeded. The highly-publicized court case dragged out for nine years, eventually resulting in an injunction against the Pirates and a financial judgement that was never collected by Disney. Dan returned to newspaper comics with his *Dan O'Neill* strip that continues today in *The San Francisco Bay Guardian* and other papers.

Dan's "The Man Who Could Work Miracles" appears in
Graphic Classics: H.G. Wells

GEORGE SELLAS (page 61)

George Sellas is a freelance cartoonist and illustrator from Cheshire, Connecticut. He is a graduate of Paier College of Art in Hamden, Connecticut with a BFA in Illustration. His work has appeared in *Highlights* magazine and in *How to Draw Those Bodacious Bad Babes of Comics* by Frank McLaughlin and Mike Gold. Mark Twain's "Tom Sawyer Abroad" was his first full-length comics story. "I'm always looking for more work to whet my artistic appetite," says George. He is now working on an adaptation of Stanley Weinbaum's "A Martian Odyssey" for the upcoming *Science Fiction Classics*.

You can get more info and view an extensive gallery of George's illustrations at www.georgesellas.com, and find his work in
Graphic Classics: Mark Twain
Graphic Classics: Robert Louis Stevenson

TODD LOVERING (page 62)

Todd was born on the East coast, and "moved out to the Northwest at 21 years of age, took a few classes at the School of Visual Art and stuck my feet into illustration. Got out and into throwing pizza. A dear friend turned me on to the video game industry and I've been working in it to this day." Todd is also an editorial and commercial illustrator and has shown his paintings in several galleries in the Northwest. He says his strongest influences are Robert Williams, Rick Griffin, Jamie Burton, Jim Blanchard and "all the talented cats I work with."

Todd's interpretation of "The Raven" appears in
Graphic Classics: Edgar Allan Poe

DEVON DEVEREAUX (page 64)

Painter and illustrator Devon Devereaux lives in Portland, Oregon. He has self-published a comics adaptation of Poe's *The Oblong Box* and also *the children*, which he describes as "kind of like Lovecraft meets *Saved by the Bell*." Devon has recently illustrated a book written by David Quinn, titled *The Littlest Bitch*. You can see more of his work at www.devondevereaux.com.

P.S. MUELLER (page 66)

P.S. Mueller has published cartoons in *The New Yorker*, *Harper's*, *Men's Journal*, *The Chicago Reader*, *Utne*, *Barron's*, *Field and Stream*, *Funny Times* and numerous alternative and mainstream magazines and newspapers over the past thirty years. Mueller also lives a double life as Doyle Redland, anchoring the syndicated *Onion Radio News*. In 2000 he co-wrote and co-produced *The Blue God*, a music CD with fellow *Graphic Classics* contributor Andy Ewen. His short prose appears occasionally in *Funny Times* and regularly in *Rosebud*. Mueller says he and his wife, artist Debra Gottschalk, are "ruled entirely by cats" in Madison, Wisconsin.

CHAD CARPENTER (page 67)

Chad Carpenter is best known for both his long-running Alaskan newspaper strip *TUNDRA*. In the sixteen years Chad has been drawing *TUNDRA*, he has compiled books, T-shirts, calendars, mouse pads, note cards and "anything else I can make a buck on," all available at www.tundracomics.com. Having lived in Alaska for thirty years, Chad says he has used the mental fatigue caused by the cold, dark winters to his advantage. It is because of these unique conditions that he is able to sit in his cabin, mumble to his imaginary friends and create wonderfully witty comic strips.

Chad and Mort Castle's biography of R.L. Stevenson is in
Graphic Classics: Robert Louis Stevenson

EVERT GERADTS (page 68)

Evert Geradts is a Dutch comics artist now living in Toulouse, France. One of the founders of the Dutch underground comix scene, he started the influential magazine *Tante Leny Presents*, in which appeared his first *Sailears & Susie* stories. He is a disciple of Carl Barks, whom he names "the Aesop of the 20th century." Over the years Geradts has written about a thousand stories featuring Donald Duck and other Disney characters for Dutch comics. He also writes stories for the popular comic series *Sjors & Sjimmie* and *De Muziekbuurters*.

Evert's work appears in
Graphic Classics: Edgar Allan Poe
Graphic Classics: Bram Stoker
Fantasy Classics: Graphic Classics Volume Fifteen

ROGER LANGRIDGE (page 70)

New Zealand-born artist Roger Langridge is the creator of Fred the Clown, whose online comics appear at www.hotelfred.com. Fred also shows up in print in *Fred the Clown* comics. With his brother Andrew, Roger's first comics series was *Zoot!* published in 1988 and recently reissued as *Zoot Suite*. Other titles followed, including *Knuckles, The Malevolent Nun* and *Art d'Ecco*. Roger's work has also appeared in numerous magazines in Britain, the U.S., France and Japan, including *Deadline, Judge Dredd, Heavy Metal, Comic Afternoon, Gross Point* and *Batman: Legends of the Dark Knight*. Roger now lives in London, where he divides his time between comics, children's books and commercial illustration.

See more comics by Roger in
Graphic Classics: Edgar Allan Poe
Graphic Classics: Arthur Conan Doyle
Graphic Classics: Jack London
Graphic Classics: Robert Louis Stevenson
Graphic Classics: Rafael Sabatini

SIMON GANE (page 72)

British artist Simon Gane lives and works in Bath. His first published strips appeared in the self-produced punk fanzine *Arnie*, and others followed in numerous mini-comics. Recent titles include *All Flee*, a comic about a "finishing school for monsters" and *Paris*, penned by Andi Watson and released by SLG Publishing. He currently pencils the DC/Vertigo series *Vinyl Underground*.

Examples can be found at www.simongane.com and in
Graphic Classics: Arthur Conan Doyle
Graphic Classics: H.G. Wells
Graphic Classics: H.P. Lovecraft
Graphic Classics: Mark Twain
Graphic Classics: Robert Louis Stevenson
Graphic Classics: Special Edition

WILLIAM L. BROWN (page 73)

Political cartoonist and illustrator William L. Brown is the author of *President Bill, A Graphic Epic*, and the continuing syndicated cartoon *Citizen Bill*. His illustration clients include *The Washington Post*, *The Wall Street Journal*, *Slate* online magazine, *The Los Angeles Times* and *The Progressive*. He works in scratchboard, digitally adding color and grey tones. He cites as influences William Morris, John Held, Jr., and the British cartoonist Giles. Bill lives in Takoma Park, Maryland, a suburb of Washington, D.C., with his wife and two children.

View more of his work at www.wmlbrown.com, and in
Graphic Classics: Mark Twain

ANTON EMDIN (page 74)

"Sailing his drawing board in a sea of India ink," Anton produces illustrations and comic art for a variety of books, magazines, websites and advertising agencies, both in Australia (where he resides) and internationally. Aside from the necessary commercial work, Anton contributes his weirdo comic art to underground comix anthologies, both in Australia and overseas, as well as self-publishing his own mini-comic, the now-sleeping ("soon, my pretties") Cruel World.

Find Anton's work at www.antongraphics.com, and in
Graphic Classics: Edgar Allan Poe
Graphic Classics: Robert Louis Stevenson

LANCE TOOKS (page 76)

As an animator for fifteen years, as well as a comics artist, Lance Tooks' work has appeared in more than a hundred television commercials, films and music videos. He has self-published the comics Divided by Infinity Danger Funnies and Muthafucka. His stories have appeared in Zuzu, Shade, Vibe, Girltalk, World War 3 Illustrated, Floaters, Pure Friction and the Italian magazine Lupo Alberto. He also illustrated The Black Panthers for Beginners, written by Herb Boyd. Lance's first graphic novel, Narcissa, was named one of the best books of 2002 by Publisher's Weekly, and he has recently completed his Lucifer's Garden of Verses series for NBM ComicsLit. In 2004 Lance moved from his native New York to Madrid, Spain, where he married and has recently finished a Spanish translation of Narcissa.

His stories appear in
Graphic Classics: Edgar Allan Poe
Graphic Classics: Mark Twain
Graphic Classics: Robert Louis Stevenson
Fantasy Classics: Graphic Classics Volume Fourteen

LISA K. WEBER (page 78)

Lisa is a graduate of Parsons School of Design in New York City, where she is currently employed in the fashion industry, designing prints and characters for teenage girls' jammies, while freelancing work on children's books and character design for animation. Other projects include her "creaturized" opera posters and playing cards which can be seen online at www.creatureco.com.

Lisa has provided comics and illustrations for
Graphic Classics: Edgar Allan Poe
Graphic Classics: H.P. Lovecraft
Graphic Classics: Mark Twain
Graphic Classics: O. Henry
Gothic Classics: Graphic Classics Volume Fourteen

JOHNNY RYAN (page 79)

Johnny Ryan was born in Boston in 1970. As a boy, he says, "first I wanted to be a cartoonist, then I wanted to be a physicist, then I wanted to be gay, and then a cartoonist again." He now lives in Los Angeles and is the creator of the award-winning Angry Youth Comix. His work has also been published in Nickelodeon Magazine, Goody Good Comics, Measles and LCD. "Comics used to be fun and crazy and weird and gross," says Johnny. "Now, they're a serious art form... it's as if everyone was having a big crazy orgy and then your grandparents walked in. They really sucked the life out of the party."

Johnny's interpretation of "The Whole Duty of Children" appears in
Graphic Classics: Robert Louis Stevenson

ANNIE OWENS (page 81)

Annie was born in Alabama, "parcel posted to the Philippines," and after three years was returned to the States and educated in the San Francisco Bay area where she earned her BFA in film and video. She is a fan of old horror films, the art of Charles Addams and Edward Gorey, and the writings of Roald Dahl, Edgar Allan Poe and H.P. Lovecraft. Samples of Annie's comic strip Ouchclub can be seen at www.ouchclub.com in Attaboy's comic anthology, I Hate Cartoons, Volume II. With Attaboy she also co-edits Hi-Fructose magazine.

Her work also appears in
Graphic Classics: Edgar Allan Poe
Graphic Classics: Mark Twain

MILTON KNIGHT (page 90)

Milton Knight claims he started drawing, painting and creating his own attempts at comic books and animation at age two. "I've never formed a barrier between fine art and cartooning," says Milton. "Growing up, I treasured Chinese watercolors, Breughel, Charlie Brown and Terrytoons equally." His work has appeared in magazines including Heavy Metal, High Times, National Lampoon and Nickelodeon Magazine, and he has illustrated record covers, posters, candy packaging and T-shirts, and occasionally exhibited his paintings. Labor on Ninja Turtles comics allowed him to get up a grubstake to move to the West Coast in 1991, where he became an animator and director on Felix the Cat cartoons. Milton's comics titles include Midnite the Rebel Skunk and Slug and Ginger, and his adaptation of Rafael Sabatini's "The Fool's Love Story" features characters from his long-running series Hugo.

More comics and illustrations by Milton Knight appear at www.miltonknight.net and in
Graphic Classics: Edgar Allan Poe
Graphic Classics: H.G. Wells
Graphic Classics: Jack London
Graphic Classics: O. Henry
Graphic Classics: Rafael Sabatini
Horror Classics: Graphic Classics Volume Ten
Adventure Classics: Graphic Classics Volume Twelve
Graphic Classics: Special Edition

RICHARD VOSS (page 100)

Der Mönch von Berchtesgaden was written by Richard Voss, and first published in 1890 in a German periodical. It was there discovered by a German immigrant to America named Gustav Adolf Danziger. Danziger translated the story to English, but was unable to find an American publisher. He brought the story to Ambrose Bierce, and asked him to polish the translation and add the prestige of his name. Bierce published "The Monk and the Hangman's Daughter" serially in The San Francisco Examiner in 1891. It was originally credited as by "Dr. G.A. Danziger and Ambrose Bierce," but when later collected in book form Bierce assumed the principal authorship. The relative contributions of Bierce and Danziger to Voss' original have long been debated, though today it stands as one of Bierce's finest contributions and among the most famous stories of the 19th century.

TOM POMPLUN

The designer, editor and publisher of Graphic Classics, Tom has a background in both fine and commercial art and a lifelong interest in comics. He designed and produced Rosebud, a journal of fiction, poetry and illustration, from 1993 to 2003, and in 2001 he founded Graphic Classics. Tom is currently working on Graphic Classics: Oscar Wilde, scheduled for December 2008 release. The book will feature a new comics adaptation of The Picture of Dorian Gray by British writer Alex Burrows and illustrated by Graphic Classics regular Lisa K. Weber, along with Wilde's play Salome, adapted by Tom and illustrated by Molly Kiely.